T0207479

Communications
in Computer and Information Science 1987

Rationale

The CCIS series is devoted to the publication of proceedings of computer science conferences. Its aim is to efficiently disseminate original research results in informatics in printed and electronic form. While the focus is on publication of peer-reviewed full papers presenting mature work, inclusion of reviewed short papers reporting on work in progress is welcome, too. Besides globally relevant meetings with internationally representative program committees guaranteeing a strict peer-reviewing and paper selection process, conferences run by societies or of high regional or national relevance are also considered for publication.

Topics

The topical scope of CCIS spans the entire spectrum of informatics ranging from foundational topics in the theory of computing to information and communications science and technology and a broad variety of interdisciplinary application fields.

Information for Volume Editors and Authors

Publication in CCIS is free of charge. No royalties are paid, however, we offer registered conference participants temporary free access to the online version of the conference proceedings on SpringerLink (http://link.springer.com) by means of an http referrer from the conference website and/or a number of complimentary printed copies, as specified in the official acceptance email of the event.

CCIS proceedings can be published in time for distribution at conferences or as post-proceedings, and delivered in the form of printed books and/or electronically as USBs and/or e-content licenses for accessing proceedings at SpringerLink. Furthermore, CCIS proceedings are included in the CCIS electronic book series hosted in the SpringerLink digital library at http://link.springer.com/bookseries/7899. Conferences publishing in CCIS are allowed to use Online Conference Service (OCS) for managing the whole proceedings lifecycle (from submission and reviewing to preparing for publication) free of charge.

Publication process

The language of publication is exclusively English. Authors publishing in CCIS have to sign the Springer CCIS copyright transfer form, however, they are free to use their material published in CCIS for substantially changed, more elaborate subsequent publications elsewhere. For the preparation of the camera-ready papers/files, authors have to strictly adhere to the Springer CCIS Authors' Instructions and are strongly encouraged to use the CCIS LaTeX style files or templates.

Abstracting/Indexing

CCIS is abstracted/indexed in DBLP, Google Scholar, EI-Compendex, Mathematical Reviews, SCImago, Scopus. CCIS volumes are also submitted for the inclusion in ISI Proceedings.

How to start

To start the evaluation of your proposal for inclusion in the CCIS series, please send an e-mail to ccis@springer.com.

Sivaram Ponnusamy · Vibha Rajesh Bora
Editors

The Role of AI in Bio-Medical Translations' Research for the Health Care Industry

First International Conference, AIBTR 2023
Nagpur, India, September 23, 2023
Revised Selected Papers

Editors
Sivaram Ponnusamy ⓘ
G H Raisoni College of Engineering
Nagpur, Maharashtra, India

Vibha Rajesh Bora ⓘ
G H Raisoni College of Engineering
Nagpur, Maharashtra, India

ISSN 1865-0929   ISSN 1865-0937 (electronic)
Communications in Computer and Information Science
ISBN 978-3-031-49453-6   ISBN 978-3-031-49454-3 (eBook)
https://doi.org/10.1007/978-3-031-49454-3

This Springer imprint is published by the registered company Springer Nature Switzerland AG
The registered company address is: Gewerbestrasse 11, 6330 Cham, Switzerland

Paper in this product is recyclable.

Preface

As editors, we are delighted to present this 1st International Conference on the Role of AI in Bio-Medical Translations' Research for the Health Care Industry (AIBTR 2023), which was organized by the Center of Excellence in Biomedical Engineering and Technology Incubation Centre (BETiC-GHRCE) and Artificial Intelligence & Machine Learning, G H Raisoni College of Engineering, Nagpur, India. The event was clinically supported by AIIMS, Nagpur, and technically sponsored by GHR Labs and Research Centre. Recent artificial intelligence (AI) breakthroughs have opened exciting new doors for businesses of all stripes. Healthcare is at the forefront of change and innovation compared to other industries. This innovative partnership between AI and healthcare is exemplified by AIBTR 2023, where top researchers worldwide gathered to discuss how AI is changing the face of medical practice. Artificial intelligence (AI) applications in biomedical translational research are crucial to reaching discoveries that may alter healthcare in this era of rapid scientific and technological advancement. This conference (AIBTR 2023) provided a worldwide forum for academics, medical professionals, government officials, and business executives to discuss how artificial intelligence (AI) might be used to improve healthcare delivery and patient outcomes.

In AIBTR 2023, we received 76 papers, and 37 papers were shortlisted for review. The double-blinded reviews were conducted with three reviewers for each paper. Focusing on the highest quality of contributions, a total of seven papers were selected. Of these, six papers were presented on 23rd September 2023. We, the editors, express our deepest gratitude to the authors for their dedication, the peer reviewers for their rigorous scrutiny, and the readers for their curiosity and commitment to pushing the boundaries of knowledge. Together, we embark on a journey to usher in a new era of "Patient-Centric: Role of AI in Bio-Medical Translational Research for the Health Care Industry," guided by the principles of innovation, precision, and compassion.

Chapter(s) Overview:

Chapter 1 investigates a vital component of our study. The authors examine the intersection of two important ideas—hyperparameter optimization and quantization techniques—within the framework of MobileNet topologies to improve diagnostic accuracy in medical picture categorization. This research investigates new approaches to increase precision when classifying medical images. To meet the unique challenges of medical image processing, the authors provide a revised version of the MobileNet architecture, a widespread neural network known for its efficiency and lightweight construction. Together, these parts offer a holistic framework that improves diagnostic accuracy in medical picture categorization and makes the model deployable on resource-constrained devices, both necessary for broader clinical use. Their study is a springboard for future research and development at the crossroads of deep learning, medical imaging, and healthcare.

Chapter 2 investigates the current state of knowledge in the complex field of orthopedic screw removal. Implant removal, especially screw extraction from implants, continues to be an essential and challenging element of orthopedic surgery. Removal of implanted screws in the event of infection, implant loosening, or other problems is crucial to the overall effectiveness of orthopedic procedures. Our goal in doing this systematic review was to provide orthopedic surgeons and other healthcare providers with a resource to help them make better clinical choices and ultimately benefit their patients.

Chapter 3 focuses on the nuanced GSDRC-Stacking-Anchor Model's potential as a helpful tool in diabetes prediction by appreciating its underlying methodology, experimental settings, and outcomes. By offering a comprehensive picture of how diverse data modalities and machine learning algorithms might be integrated to handle a challenging health issue, this study provides an essential addition to the continuing conversation in predictive medicine. The cutting-edge approach is the focus of this research. Years of research and development into machine learning techniques for diabetes prediction have led to the findings presented in this paper. This article aims to provide readers with information and motivation to explore the promising intersection of healthcare and data science.

Chapter 4 presents the improved techniques of diagnosis and therapy for low back pain (LBP) that are possible due to new results and approaches which will help us better understand the reasons for gait irregularities in patients with LBP. The intricacy and coordination necessary to evaluate gait have piqued the curiosity of researchers, medics, and healthcare professionals for decades. An individual's motor function, musculoskeletal health, and overall health and well-being may all be gleaned by analyzing their gait data. There is mounting evidence that utilizing image processing technologies to assess and detect gait constraints may improve our understanding of various medical conditions, from LBP to dementia.

Chapter 5 explores a significant new perspective in the ongoing debate over whether or not blockchain technology can enhance healthcare security. It is the product of a collaborative effort to provide a framework for improving user-controlled access inside a secure, private, and confidential healthcare IT environment. Safeguarding patients' privacy while giving them simple access to their medical information has been a long-standing challenge for the healthcare informatics community. The "MediSecure" architecture balances allowing consumers complete access to their data and providing the most significant privacy possible using blockchain technology and ensemble learning techniques. The authors want to spark new inquiries, collaborations, and discussions by publishing their results, resulting in a more secure and confidential future for medical cyber-physical systems.

Chapter 6 discusses the combination of two state-of-the-art approaches: the Faster Region-based Convolutional Neural Networks (Faster RCNNs) and the Kai-Bi-Directional Long Short-Term Memory Networks (Kai-Bi-LSTMs). Due to the advantage of faster RCNNs in extracting salient features from pictures, the model can detect delicate details and structures within skeletal radiographs. However, a version of LSTM dubbed Kai-Bi-LSTM appears beneficial for processing and analyzing natural language inquiries users ask regarding the photos. In light of this, this essay is produced with the expectation that it will stimulate more thought and investigation into the use of AI in healthcare and diagnostics.

These chapter overviews give readers a taste of the wide range of topics discussed at AIBTR 2023, which includes research into finite-element analysis and topology optimization, better methods of diagnosis and treatment for LBP, applying artificial intelligence to healthcare and diagnostics, AI-assisted orthopedic screw removal, AI-assisted real-world medical picture classification, AI with blockchain for patients' privacy, and data-driven diabetic prediction. The papers all add to our knowledge of the role of AI in biomedical, translational research, and the healthcare sector as a whole.

Finally, we'd like to thank everyone who contributed to AIBTR 2023 for their hard work. Our sincere thanks go to Springer Nature. This collection would not exist without their hard work and knowledge. This AIBTR 2023 proceedings volume aims to be an invaluable tool for scientists, professionals, and enthusiasts in computer science, artificial intelligence, and biomedical translations by stimulating them to probe uncharted territory in the study of the latter.

December 2023   Sivaram Ponnusamy
                                                      Vibha Rajesh Bora

Organization

Program Committee Chairs

Sivaram Ponnusamy	G H Raisoni College of Engineering, India
Vibha Rajesh Bora	G H Raisoni College of Engineering, India

Program Co-chair

Juwono F.	University of Southampton, Malaysia

Patrons

Sunil Raisoni	Raisoni Group of Institutions, India
Shobha Raisoni	Raisoni Group of Institutions, India
Shreyas Raisoni	Raisoni Group of Institutions, India

Honorary Chair

Sachin Untawale	G H Raisoni College of Engineering, India

Principal Conveners

Pramod Walke	G H Raisoni College of Engineering, India
Sanjay Dorle	G H Raisoni College of Engineering, India
Dinesh Padole	G H Raisoni College of Engineering, India

Organizing Chair

Santosh Jaju	G H Raisoni College of Engineering, India

General Chairs

Mangala Madankar	G H Raisoni College of Engineering, India
Laxman Thakre	G H Raisoni College of Engineering, India

International Advisory Members

Rangaraj Rangayyan	University of Calgary, Canada
Vincenzo Piuri	University of Milan, Italy
James Geller	New Jersey Institute of Technology, USA
Bingyun Bing Li	West Virginia University, USA
Jilali Antari	Ibn Zohr University, Morocco
Paulo Mazzoncini de Azevedo Marques	University of Sao Paulo, FMRP, Brazil
Balas Valentina	University of Arad, Romania
Arianna Mencattini	University of Rome, Italy
Sridhar Krishnan	Toronto Metropolitan University, Canada
Faraz Oloumi	University of Calgary, Canada

National Advisory Members

Mukesh Doble	IIT Madras, India
Rathna G. N.	IISc Bengaluru, India
Rohit Srivastava	IIT Bombay, India
Renu John	IIT Hyderabad, India
Rambilas Pachori	IIT Indore, India
Darshan Shah	IIT Bombay, India
Rupesh Ghyar	IIT Bombay, India
Abhay Kuthe	Visvesvaraya National Institute of Technology Nagpur, India
Mrunal Phatak	AIIMS Nagpur, India
Hemanth Jude	Karunya University, India

Organizing Committee

Sonali Joshi	G H Raisoni College of Engineering, India
Wani Patil	G H Raisoni College of Engineering, India
Achamma Thomas	G H Raisoni College of Engineering, India
Priti Gade	G H Raisoni College of Engineering, India

Payal Ghutke	G H Raisoni College of Engineering, India
Trushna Deotale	G H Raisoni College of Engineering, India
Parul Dubey	G H Raisoni College of Engineering, India
Pranali Dhawas	G H Raisoni College of Engineering, India
Swati Paraskar	G H Raisoni College of Engineering, India
Manisha Raut	G H Raisoni College of Engineering, India
Swati Sorte	G H Raisoni College of Engineering, India
Rucha Jichkar	G H Raisoni College of Engineering, India
Krupali Dhawale	G H Raisoni College of Engineering, India
Dhananjay Bhagat	G H Raisoni College of Engineering, India
Shyam Bhawankar	G H Raisoni College of Engineering, India
Manthan Ghosh	G H Raisoni College of Engineering, India
Minakshi Ramteke	G H Raisoni College of Engineering, India

Reviewers

Kevin Hung
Antari Jilali
Rathna G. N.
Amol Rahulkar
Ashwin Kothari
Vishal Satpute
Manish Kurhekar
Ankit Bhurane
Saugata Sinha
Vipin Kamble
Paritosh Peshwe
John Basha Mohamed Basha
Shailendra Aote
Nikhil Dhengre
Sushil Mankar
Omkar Vaidya
Lenin V. R.
Nidhya Rangarajan
Bharati Ainapure
Amit Lathigara
Rajesh A.
Archana Ratnaparakhi

Murugesan Sundaram
Rajeev Shrivastava
Sanjay Pokle
Yogita Dubey
Anish Vishwakarma
Prachi Palsodkar
Mythili Shanmugam
Swaminathan Kalyanaraman
Ravi Tiwari
Sandhya M. K.
Rajesh Raut
Sandhyarani Shirsat
Rashmi Mahajan
Ganesh Khekare
Nikhil Marriwala
Sandip Desai
Naresh R.
Selvaraj Ayyaakkannu
Sourabh Paul
Sonali Joshi
Tushar Barai

Contents

A Novel Hyperparameter Optimized Quantized MobileNet Architecture
for Improving Diagnostic Accuracy in the Medical Image Classification 1
Rupa Patel and Anita Chaware

A Systematical Review of the Literature on Screw Extraction from Implants
During Orthopedic Surgery 14
Pramar Bakane and S. B. Jaju

Analytic Algorithm for Predicting Diabetes Based
on GSDRC-Stacking-Anchor Model 39
Jiaxin Jiang and Yanhui Zhou

Detection and Analysis of Gait Impairments in Lower Back Pain (LBP)
Patients Using Image Processing Techniques 55
P. Praveen, M. S. Mallikarjunaswamy, and S. Chandrashekara

MediSecure: A Blockchain-Enabled Ensemble Learning Approach
for User-Controlled Single Sign-On and Privacy Preservation in Medical
Cyber-Physical Systems 71
Jagdish F. Pimple, Avinash Sharma, and Jitendra Kumar Mishra

Visual Question Answering System for Skeletal Images Based on Feature
Extraction Using Faster RCNN and Kai-Bi-LSTM Techniques 87
Y. I. Jinesh Melvin, Sushopti Gawade, and Mukesh Shrimali

Author Index 103

A Novel Hyperparameter Optimized Quantized MobileNet Architecture for Improving Diagnostic Accuracy in the Medical Image Classification

Rupa Patel[1]([⊠]) [iD] and Anita Chaware[2] [iD]

[1] Research Scholar, P.G. Department of Computer Science. S.N.D.T.W.U, Asst. Professor, Department of Information Technology, Anna Leela College of Commerce and Economics, Mumbai, India
rupalearn1@gmail.com
[2] Department of Computer Science. S.N.D.T.W.U, Mumbai, India
Anita.Chaware@computerc.sndt.ac.in

Abstract. In recent years, there is a remarkable use of smartphones in the field of computer vision. Deep convolutional neural networks being the backbone of computer vision has forced the DCNN to mitigate from heavyweight network to lightweight network. Smartphones are resource constrained devices with limited storage and processing capabilities. DCNN, a heavyweight network, cannot be implemented directly on such devices. We require a lightweight version for smartphones that meets the desirable properties such as small model size and acceptable accuracy. DCNN can be compressed using the neural network quantization process. But the quantization process introduces quantization error that degrades the accuracy. In this paper we propose a novel hyperparameter optimization of quantized deep convolutional architecture that mitigates quantization loss while maintaining the competing accuracy.

The performance of HPOQ-MobileNet is tested and verified for image classification tasks on Diabetic Retinopathy dataset. The accuracy of the baseline model is 83.81% and that of proposed HPOQ-MobileNetv2 architecture is 82.9%. The inference accuracy of fine-tuned Mobilenetv1 is 81.8% and that of proposed HPOQ-MobileNetv1 model is 80.3%. The proposed architecture shows optimized accuracy and effective resource utilization by reducing the memory footprint by 4×, and quantization loss approximately by 1%. Quantization simulation shows that the model can be ported to resource constrained devices.

Keywords: Quantization · MobileNetv2 · Hyperparameter · Optimization · Deep Neural Network

1 Introduction

Recent advancements in Convolutional neural network architecture have focused on effective resource utilization in terms of memory, energy consumption and computational speed. Deep Convolutional Neural Networks have a high processing rate and demand a

S. Ponnusamy and V. R. Bora (Eds.): AIBTR 2023, CCIS 1987, pp. 1–13, 2024.
https://doi.org/10.1007/978-3-031-49454-3_1

big amount of memory, making them difficult to implement on limited resources. As a result, it is critical to lower both the computational and memory costs for such devices [1].

The model's complexity is greatly reduced through neural network compression techniques. Network compression methods include Knowledge distillation, Pruning and Quantization [2]. Quantization process involves changing the representation of weights from higher precision to lower [3]. On existing DCNN models such as VGG16 [7], RESNET [8], MobileNet [9, 10] inference accuracy is compromised after quantization [11]. This research work focuses on obtaining a lightweight neural network that is as small, computational efficient and achieves acceptable accuracy.

One of the approaches to optimize the network is through hyperparameter tuning. They play a crucial role in defining the architecture and behavior of the model during training. The hyper parameters such as activation functions, kernel size, stride, number of hidden layers and padding are used to calculate model parameters (weight and bias). Learning rate, batch size, number of epoch, dropout rate and optimizer are used to control the behavior of training algorithm [13, 14, 15].

The hyperparameters can be tuned in a variety of ways to boost the network's performance. In the manual approach, the hyperparameters are manually selected using a method known as trial and error. Grid search [12], random search [13, 16], Bayesian optimization [14], and evolutionary optimization [15] are among the various automatic approaches.

The main contribution of the work highlighted in this paper can be summed up as follows:

1. The following challenges are intended to be addressed by proposed architecture. Need of Compressed model for resource constrained devices with competing accuracy.
2. The effectiveness of the suggested strategy has been demonstrated in optimizing hyperparameters of quantized models.
3. The proposed approach is also applicable in the Medical domain where the dataset is limited.

The remainder of this paper is composed of the following sections. Background information can be found in Sect. 2. The planned architecture is covered in Sect. 3. Experimental findings are reviewed and compared with relevant work in Sect. 4. The paper is concluded in Sect. 5.

2 Background

2.1 Neural Network Compression

Neural network compression refers to the methods used for reducing a neural network model's size or complexity while minimizing its impact on performance. The main goals of neural network compression is to reduce the parameters counts, the memory footprint of the network and computational complexity of the model making it deployable on the resource constrained device.

Network Pruning, Quantization, knowledge distillation are the compression techniques [2]. The pruning process reduces redundant features such as weights, neurons, filters or channels from the network. Unstructured Pruning involves removing weights or neurons. Pruning weight decreases the number of parameters without affecting the architecture. Structured pruning removes filters or channels from the network [18]. Quantization refers to the process of representing 32 bit floating point (FP32) by lower precision [2]. However, this mapping can also introduce quantization errors, which can affect the accuracy of the neural network. To minimize the impact of quantization errors scaling factors are used [18, 19, 20, 21].The two main quantization approaches are quantization aware training and post-training. Knowledge distillation techniques deal with training a small network from a large pretrained network by transferring knowledge [2].

2.2 Optimization

The objective of hyperparameter optimization is to find the set of network hyperparameters that maximizes the performance metric [22] on the validation set.

$$P \text{ (score | optimal set of hyperparameter)} \tag{1}$$

where Score represent the accuracy of model, given input a set of hyperparameter.

The proposed optimization algorithm optLOBADE () uses a search strategy to find the optimal set of hyperparameters for a network. First identify the set of hyperparameters (optimizer, activation function, learning rate, dropout, batch size, and epoch) and then define the set of values for each hyperparameter. The following are the detailed steps of the algorithm.

Algorithm 1: optLOBADE (Inputs) **returns** best combination of set of hyperparameter values

Inputs: Opt –Optimizer (ADAM, SGD)
                LR- Learning rate (0.1, 0.001, 0.002, 0.00002)
                ACT-Activation Function (RELU, Softmax)
                Dp – dropout (0.2, 0.5)
                BS –Batch Size (8, 16, 32, 64)
                Epoch-(10, 20, 30, 40)

    a. For each value in Opt do
          i. For each value in LR do
         ii. For each value in Dp do
       iii. For each value in BS do
       iv. For epoch in range(10,40,10)
               1. Train the network
               2. Store the accuracy
               3. Save the set of hyperparameter values
    b. Compare the accuracy of models (obtained in step a.)
    c. Save the best model for set of hyperparameter

Output: Optimal set of Hyperparameters.

3 Proposed Work

The Algorithm 2 illustrates the steps involved in the proposed approach. The objective of the approach is to create an architecture that will reduce quantization loss and improve accuracy. The first step is to preprocess the dataset. Step 2 quantized the weights of the network. Step 3 trains the network with quantized weights. Quantization loss is recorded. In Step 4 the network is fine-tuned to compensate for the loss using optLOBADE () algorithm. Step 5 use HPO-MobileNet for inference accuracy with test data.

Algorithm 2: The Proposed Method
Purpose: Construct an optimized quantized MobileNet model

Step 1: Dataset Preparation
  - Resize the image to desired size (224 x 224).
  - Dataset is divided into training data and validation sets.

Step 2: Quantization of MobileNet
  - Fine tune pretrained MobileNet model
  - The weights of the network are quantized from their original floating-point representation to a fixed-point representation with reduced precision. This involves applying a quantization function to each weight parameter.

$$Q(x) = round(x / s) * s \qquad (2)$$

  Here, $Q(x)$ represents the quantized value of the weight parameter x, and s represents the scaling factor that determines the quantization granularity.

Step 3: Train the network with quantized weights
.
Step 4: Optimize the Network
  - Finding the set of network hyperparameters that maximizes the accuracy is the goal of this step. One way to formulate this is , is as an optimization problem:

$$\lambda_H = optLOBADE(Inputs: Hyperparameters) \qquad (3)$$

  Where λ_H is the optimal set of hyperparameters.

Step 5: Approaches for testing new test data
  - In step 4 the best combination of hyperparameters have been selected to train the quantized model built in step3.
  - For new data sets, retrain the network.

Output: Optimized Quantized MobileNet model

The suggested algorithm's mathematical perspective can be represented as follows:

$$max_{accuracy} = \left\{ \lambda_H \left[\prod_{ij} \frac{1}{Sw_{ik}} \cdot \frac{1}{Sx_{kj}} \sum_k Q(w, \partial w).Q(v, \partial v) + b \right] \right\} \quad (4)$$

where

$max_{accuracy}$- Maximize accuracy.

Sw_{ik}, Sx_{kj}– Scaling factor that maps the floating point (fp32) range (fp$_{max}$, fp$_{min}$) to lower precision range to (l$_{max}$, l$_{min}$). Sw_{ik} Factor is used for mapping weights. And Sx_{kj} for input data respectively. Scaling factor is expressed as [21]

$$S = \frac{(fp_{max} - fp_{min})}{(l_{max} - l_{min})} \quad (5)$$

∂w and $\partial v-are$ the quantization parameters used in quantization function for weights and input vector respectively.

b – bias.

λ_H - Optimal hyperparameter combination that balances the quantization loss.

4   Experimental Results and Discussion

This section presents the results obtained through our proposed approach. The experiments were conducted with baseline MobileNet, quantized MobileNet and HPOQ-MobileNet on Diabetic Retinopathy dataset from Kaggle -APTOS 2019 blindness detection. If undetected and untreated, diabetic retinopathy (DR), a complication of diabetes that affects the eyes, can cause blindness [23]. The dataset contains a total of 3,662 retinal images which were divided into a training set and a validation set (80:20). Each image in the dataset is associated with a severity level of diabetic retinopathy, which is graded on a scale from 0 to 4. The severity levels represent the following categories along with the number of images in those categories [24]:

0: No diabetic retinopathy (1850).
1: Mild diabetic retinopathy (370).
2: Moderate diabetic retinopathy (999).
3: Severe diabetic retinopathy (193).
4: Proliferative diabetic retinopathy (295).

The architecture was trained on the training set and evaluated on the validation set for N number of epochs. The performance of the proposed approach was evaluated using accuracy. The Classification accuracy and the loss for baseline FP32 Mobilenetv1 is illustrated, accordingly, in Table 1 and Fig. 1.

The model is quantized to INT8 architecture. The performance is observed. Table 2 and Fig. 2 shows the INT8 Mobilenetv1 classification accuracy and loss respectively.

Table 1. FP32 MobileNetV1 Classification Accuracy

	Training		Validation	
No. of Epoch	Accuracy	Loss	Accuracy	Loss
10	0.6915	0.9162	0.5409	0.8618
30	0.8962	0.6502	0.7820	0.6492
50	0.9568	0.3452	0.8183	0.4757

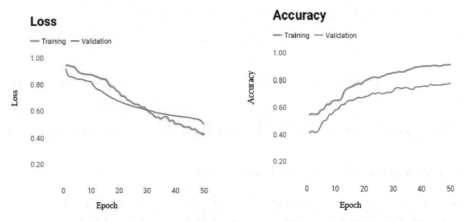

Fig. 1. Classification Loss and Accuracy of FP32 MobileNetV1

Table 2. INT8 MobileNetv1 classification Accuracy and Loss

	Training		Validation	
No. of Epoch	Accuracy	Loss	Accuracy	Loss
10	0.5937	0.8223	0.4676	0.9316
30	0.7224	0.5895	0.7408	0.6397
50	0.8010	0.3031	0.7708	0.4922

To enhance the quantized model's efficiency optimization technique is implemented. Table 3 and Fig. 3 shows the outcome of HPOQ-MobileNetv1 classification accuracy and loss respectively.

Similar experiments were performed with MobileNetv2 architecture. Table 4 and Fig. 4 shows the classification accuracy and loss for baseline FP32 Mobilenetv2 respectively.

Table 5 and Fig. 5 respectively show the INT8 Mobilenetv2 classification accuracy and loss.

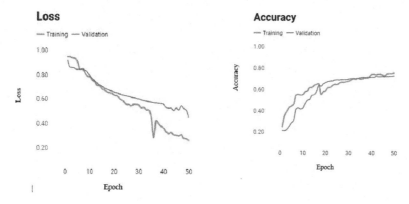

Fig. 2. INT8 MobileNetv1 classification Loss and Accuracy

Table 3. HPOQ-MobileNetv1 classification Loss and Accuracy

	Training		Validation	
No. of Epoch	Accuracy	Loss	Accuracy	Loss
10	0.7791	0.5895	0.7831	0.5966
30	0.9054	0.2541	0.7736	0.3462
50	0.9789	0.1315	0.8072	0.3191

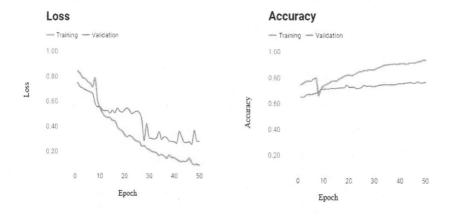

Fig. 3. HPOQ-MobileNetv1 classification Loss and Accuracy

Table 6 and Fig. 6 respectively shows the HPOQ-MobileNetv2 classification accuracy and loss.

Table 7 and Table 8 shows the validation accuracy obtained when F32, INT8 and HPOQ Models were tested for image validation dataset. With HPOQ Model the quantization loss has been significantly reduced for both MobileNetv1 and MobileNetv2.During

Table 4. Classification Accuracy of FP32 MobileNetv2

	Training		Validation	
No. of Epoch	Accuracy	Loss	Accuracy	Loss
10	0.8466	0.4146	0.7635	0.5615
30	0.9471	0.2121	0.7879	0.3223
50	0.9825	0.1249	0.8381	0.2856

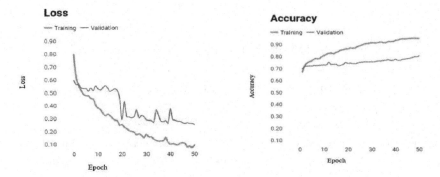

Fig. 4. Classification Loss and Accuracy of FP32 MobileNet2

Table 5. INT8 MobileNetv2 classification Accuracy and Loss

	Training		Validation	
No. of Epoch	Accuracy	Loss	Accuracy	Loss
10	0.7132	0.8223	0.7367	0.7337
30	0.7917	0.5671	0.7653	0.6112
50	0.8489	0.4201	0.7940	0.5513

the training process, the network parameters are updated to minimize the quantization loss using stochastic gradient descent.

Figure 7 depicts a comparison of the FP32 baseline's accuracy models and their quantized equivalent models. As can be seen, there is accuracy loss between the baseline and quantized models. HPOQ-MobileNet has significantly better accuracy than quantized. As shown in Fig. 8, the quantization loss for MobileNetv1 and MobileNetv2 has been greatly decreased using HPOQ-MobileNet.

Table 9 shows comparison of the suggested strategy and related works.

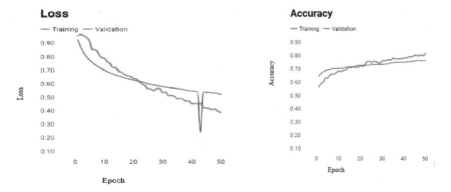

Fig. 5. INT8 MobileNetv2 classification Loss and Accuracy

Table 6. HPOQ-MobileNetv2 classification Loss and Accuracy

	Training		Validation	
No. of Epoch	Accuracy	Loss	Accuracy	Loss
10	0.7023	0.8998	0.6620	0.5075
30	0.9047	0.6189	0.7875	0.6397
50	0.9696	0.2572	0.8229	0.4731

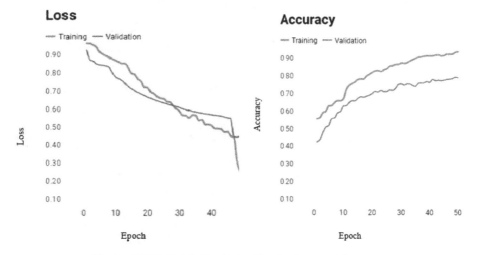

Fig. 6. HPOQ-MobileNetv2 classification Loss and Accuracy

Table 7. Comparison of MobileNetV1and proposed HPOQ-MobileNetv1

	FP32-MobileNetv1	INT8-Mobilenetv1	HPOQ-MobileNetv1
Accuracy	81.8%	77.08%	80.72%
Quantization Loss		6.1%	1.1%

Table 8. Comparison of MobileNetV2and proposed HPOQ-MobileNetV2

	FP32-MobileNetv2	INT8-Mobilenetv2	HPOQ-MobileNetv2
Accuracy	83.8%	79.40%	82.29%
Quantization Loss	-	4.8%	0.9%

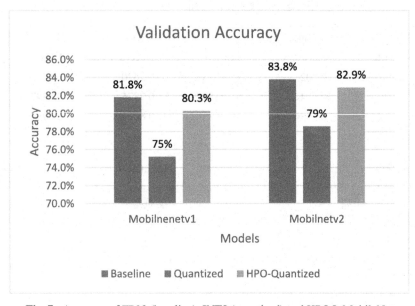

Fig. 7. Accuracy of FP32 (baseline), INT8 (quantized) and HPOQ-MobileNet

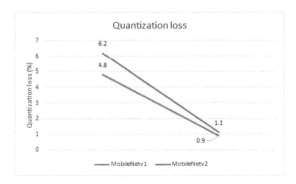

Fig. 8. Quantization loss of the Proposed HPOQ-MobileNet and Baseline MobileNet

Table 9. Comparison of Proposed work and related work

Model	Accuracy	Model	Accuracy
QF-MobileNetv2 [39]	67.81%	Quantization Friendly –MobileNetv1 [11]	68.03%
Proposed Work (HPOQ-MobileNetV2)	82.9%	Proposed Work (HPOQ-MobileNetV1)	80.72%

5   Conclusion

We have proposed a model that uses a novel combination of quantization and hyperparameter optimized technique. F32 MobileNetV2 model is quantized to the INT8 model that consumes 4x less storage as compared to FP32.Quantized MobileNet is optimized using hyperparameter optimization technique to achieve the accuracy of baseline model by minimizing the quantization loss. The accuracy of HPOQ-MobileNetv2 is 82.9% and HPOQ-MobileNetv1 is 81.8%. The accuracy is approximately the same as that of baseline models with reduced storage requirement.

HPOQ-MobileNet architecture can provide a more efficient and accurate deep learning solution for resource-constrained devices, making it easier to deploy deep learning applications in real-world scenarios.

Acknowledgments. This research did not received any specific grant.

Declarations. There is no conflict of interest.

References

1. Denil, M., Shakibi, B., Dinh, L., Ranzato, M.A., De Freitas, N.: Predicting parameters in deep learning. In: Advances in Neural Information Processing Systems, pp. 2148–2156 (2013)

2. Patel, R., Chaware, A.: Quantizing mobilenet models for classification problem. In: INDIACom-2021; 15th INDIACom; 2021 8th International Conference on "Computing for Sustainable Global Development",organised by BVICAM, New Delhi. 17th–19th March (2021)
3. Gholami, A., Kim, S., Dong, Z., Yao, Z., Mahoney, M.W., Keutzer, K.: A survey of quantization methods for efficient neural network inference. arXiv preprint arXiv:2103.13630 (2021)
4. Jin, H., et al.: Hyperparameter Importance for Machine Learning Algorithms. arXiv preprint arXiv:2201.05132 (2022)
5. Gülcü, A., Kuş, Z.: Hyper-parameter selection in convolutional neural networks using microcanonical optimization algorithm. IEEE Access **8**, 52528–52540 (2020)
6. Yang, L., Shami, A.: On hyperparameter optimization of machine learning algorithms: theory and practice. Neurocomputing **20**(415), 295–316 (2020)
7. Simonyan, K., Andrew, Z.: Very deep convolutional networks for large-scale image recognition. arXiv preprint arXiv:1409.1556 (2014)
8. He, K., Zhang, X., Ren, S. and Sun, J.: Deep residual learning for image recognition. In: Proceedings of the IEEE Conference on Computer Vision and Pattern Recognition, pp. 770–778 (2016)
9. Howard, A.G., Zhu, M., Chen, et.al.: Mobilenets: efficient convolutional neural networks for mobile vision applications (2017). arXiv preprint arXiv:1704.04861
10. Sandler, M., et al.: Mobilenetv2: inverted residuals and linear bottlenecks. In: Proceedings of the IEEE Conference on Computer Vision and Pattern Recognition (2018)
11. Sheng, T., Feng, C., Zhuo, S., Zhang, X., Shen, L., Aleksic, M.: March A quantization-friendly separable convolution for mobilenets. In: 2018 1st Workshop on Energy Efficient Machine Learning and Cognitive Computing for Embedded Applications (EMC2), pp. 14–18. IEEE (2018)
12. Lerman, P.M.: Fitting segmented regression models by grid search. J. Roy. Stat. Soc.: Ser. C (Appl. Stat.) **29**(1), 77–84 (1980)
13. James, B., Yoshua, B.: Random search for hyper-parameter optimization. J. Mach. Learn. Res. **13**(2) (2012)
14. James, B., Rémi, B., Yoshua, B., Balázs, K.: Algorithms for hyper-parameter optimization. In: Advances in Neural Information Processing Systems **24** (2011)
15. Ilya, L., Frank, H.: Cma-es for hyperparameter optimization of deep neural networks. arXiv preprint arXiv:1604.07269, 2016. Pavel Brazdil, Christophe Gi
16. Amirabadi, M.A., Kahaei, M.H., Nezamalhosseini, S.A.: Novel suboptimal approaches for hyperparameter tuning of deep neural network [under the shelf of optical communication]. Phys. Commun. **41**, 101057 (2020): 101057
17. Mockus, J.: Bayesian approach to global optimization: Theory and applications. Springer (2012)
18. Han, S., Mao, H. and Dally, W.J.: Deep compression: Compressing deep neural networks with pruning, trained quantization and huffman coding. arXiv preprint arXiv:1510.00149 (2015)
19. Nagel, M., Fournarakis, M., Bondarenko, Y., Blankevoort, T.: Overcoming oscillations in quantization-aware training. In: International Conference on Machine Learning 2022 Jun 28, pp. 16318–16330. PMLR
20. Kulkarni, U., Meena, S.M., Gurlahosur, S.V., Bhogar, G.: Quantization friendly mobilenet (QF-MobileNet) architecture for vision based applications on embedded platforms. Neural Netw. **1**(136), 28–39 (2021)
21. Wu, H., Judd, P., Zhang, X., Isaev, M. and Micikevicius, P., 2020. Integer quantization for deep learning inference: Principles and empirical evaluation. arXiv preprint arXiv:2004.09602
22. Frazier, P.I.: A tutorial on Bayesian optimization. arXiv preprint arXiv:1807.02811. 2018 Jul 8

23. https://www.kaggle.com/competitions/aptos2019-blindness-detection/data
24. Rupa, P., Anita, C.: Transfer learning with fine-tuned mobileNetV2 for diabetic retinopathy. In: 2020 International Conference for Emerging Technology (INCET) , Belgaum, India, 5–7 June 2020, pp. 1–4. IEEE. https://doi.org/10.1109/INCET49848.2020.9154014

A Systematical Review of the Literature on Screw Extraction from Implants During Orthopedic Surgery

Pramar Bakane[1]([✉]) [iD] and S. B. Jaju[2] [iD]

[1] Department of Mechanical Engineering G.H. Raisoni College of Engineering,
Nagpur, MS 440016, India
pramarbakane@gmail.com
[2] Department of Mechanical Engineering G.H. Raisoni College of Engineering,
Nagpur, MS 440016, India
santosh.jaju@raisoni.net

Abstract. Implant removal during fracture healing has always been a contentious but practical subject. Cold welding and the absence of screw heads make it difficult to remove these implants. Removing the screws associated with these complexities is, nevertheless, without doubt. Inevitably, there will come a time when such metal apparatus must be removed, and this will be done for various reasons and at different times, each of which is likely inconvenient.

Methodology: Over five years (2014–2019), a study was conducted on medical records involving the removal of musculoskeletal implants. Data on segments, clinical nuances, evacuation indicators, and post-employment challenges were collected.

Results: Thirty patients' complete medical histories were analyzed. Males outnumbered females by a ratio of 1.7 to 1, and ages varied from 6 to 76 (mean = 30.08). The femur, tibia, humerus, distal span, and clavicle were common removal sites. Nails (20.8%) and edge plates (54.2%) followed plates and screws as the most often discarded hardware (12.5%). Disease was the most frequently identified symptom, with 41.7%, followed by equipment dissatisfaction (28.6%) and patient requests (11.9%). Diseases related to work-related injuries accounted for 57% of the post-useful discomfort rate, while distress accounted for 15% and repeated fractures made up the remaining 2% (7%).

The purpose of this work is to use artificial intelligence (AI) tools to thoroughly review the available literature on screw extraction during orthopedic surgery. The ability of AI to extract knowledge, interpret data, and recognize patterns makes it an effective tool for studying enormous amounts of scientific material. This review seeks to offer a thorough overview of the most recent developments, methods, and results in relation to screw extraction operations using AI-powered algorithms.

Keywords: Artificial intelligence · broken implants · removing implants or hardware · removing implants · removing hardware

S. Ponnusamy and V. R. Bora (Eds.): AIBTR 2023, CCIS 1987, pp. 14–38, 2024.
https://doi.org/10.1007/978-3-031-49454-3_2

1   Introduction

A precise procedure called as "screw extraction" in orthopedic surgery removes screws from bone without endangering the neighboring structures. This technique can be challenging due to a number of factors, including screw size, position, bone quality, and implant type. Due to the expanding popularity of AI, its applications in the medical field have increased. A significant volume of literature might be evaluated automatically by AI systems, allowing for precise and efficient systematic reviews. This work, which includes a wide range of orthopedic operations using screw fixation, such as fracture fixation, joint arthroplasty, and spinal fusion, uses AI methodologies to conduct an extensive literature evaluation on the removal of screws during orthopedic surgery. By examining a wide spectrum of orthopedic surgeries, we aim to provide a holistic view of screw extraction challenges and solutions across different clinical scenarios. Additionally, we will explore the biomechanical aspects of screw loosening and breakage, which are critical in understanding the forces that contribute to implant failure and the subsequent need for extraction.

The science of implant removal has long been a hot subject in the field of biomechanics of internal fixation for two main reasons: (1) the rapid pace at which new and improved fixation devices are being developed and (2) the lack of a universally accepted set of criteria for their removal [2–4]. Orthopedic surgery often involves the use of implants, such as screws, to stabilize fractured bones, promote bone healing, and restore joint function. While these implants play a crucial role in enhancing patient outcomes, there are instances when they need to be removed due to various reasons, such as infection, screw loosening, non-union, or implant failure. The process of screw extraction, however, presents its own set of challenges and complexities, making it a critical aspect of orthopedic practice that demands careful consideration and investigation. The extraction of screws from orthopedic implants is a delicate procedure that requires precise planning and execution. The success of screw removal significantly impacts the overall outcome of the orthopedic surgery and the subsequent rehabilitation of the patient. Despite its importance, the knowledge surrounding screw extraction techniques is scattered across various sources, including research papers, case reports, and expert opinions. Thus, there exists a need for a comprehensive and systematic review of the literature to synthesize existing knowledge, identify gaps, and provide evidence-based insights for the improvement of screw extraction practices.

Cold welding and screw head removal might make it difficult to remove these implants [1, 5, 12]. There is little evidence available for unlocking screws [6]. It includes the use of diamond-tipped burrs, discs, and extraction screws with conical heads, as well as carbide drill bits. However, the indicators for and timing of the actual activity remain unclear [2, 4], and most of these tactics involve complicated equipment that is not immediately available to all professionals. The tension in the plate's apexes may weaken the bone or cause fissures in the plate's surface, depending on the implant's pressure [4, 5]. Pain, post-employment illness, and implant failure may result from contact between held implants and neighbouring critical structures. [5–7].On the other hand, careful removal of an implant carries an increased risk of complications such as neurovascular damage and refractures. Titanium is preferred over tempered steel, and locking compression plates have primarily replaced traditional plating systems as osteosynthesis has advanced over the last decade. The locking plating and titanium enhance osseointegration in a callus arrangement [4, 5]. Bone expansion around implant plates and screws is a potential complication of these two mechanisms [8]. The implant removal process has gotten more complicated due to the locking mechanism in these new devices. Research has focused on the advantages of LCPs for fracture fixing, but much less attention has been paid to the difficulties associated with removing them. Therefore, this research aims to compile information on implant removal procedures for those who have successfully treated their LCP obsession. Methods for safely and successfully resolving potential instances of specialized entanglements during surgical operations are studied. This study seeks to efficiently gather data on implant removal surgeries performed on patients with severe LCP addiction. It emphasizes recognizing the prevalence of specialized confusions during medical operations and safe and practical strategies for resolving them.

There are many advantages of using AI techniques to perform a thorough evaluation of the literature on the removal of screws during orthopedic surgery. AI-powered algorithms are used to make the evaluation more thorough, accurate, and efficient. The results of this review's findings can help orthopedic surgeons decide on the best screw extraction methods, enhancing patient outcomes and lowering risks.

2 Literature Review

We conduct a systematic review of the literature using AI-powered algorithms. Initially, a pre-defined search strategy is developed to identify relevant studies from databases The AI algorithms employ natural language processing techniques to extract key information from the selected studies. These algorithms can identify keywords, relevant outcomes, study designs, and technical details related to screw extraction. The extracted data is then synthesized to provide a comprehensive review of the literature.

The article [2] looks into what orthopaedic surgeons believe and think about removing orthopaedic implants after a fracture has healed. 730 participants in the AO Principles and Masters Courses in Operative Fracture Treatment in Davos, Switzerland, were given a 41-item questionnaire as part of the study. A total of 655 replies, or 54.6% of all course participants from 65 different countries, were received.The study achieved a high response rate of 89.7%, indicating a strong engagement of orthopaedic surgeons on the topic.The study includes responses from surgeons in 65 countries, providing a diverse perspective on implant removal practices worldwide. The study highlights the ongoing controversy surrounding routine implant removal. A substantial proportion of surgeons (58%) disagreed that routine removal is necessary, reflecting differing opinions on the topic. The survey provides insights into surgeons' perceptions of risks associated with implant removal. A significant percentage (48%) felt that removal is riskier than leaving the implant in situ, indicating the need for further investigation into safety concerns. The investigation found that the majority (85%) of participants acknowledged that the removal of implants could impose a strain on hospital resources, drawing attention to the potential effects on healthcare systems. However, it is important to note that the study's scope was limited to the perceptions of surgeons attending a specific course, and thus, it may not fully reflect the opinions of the wider orthopaedic community.

The study utilizes self-reported responses, which may introduce biases and inaccuracies into the results. The article highlights the absence of evidence-based guidelines regarding implant removal, underscoring the necessity for additional research to establish standardized protocols. It also indicates the importance of conducting large randomized trials to assess the efficacy and effectiveness of implant removal, taking patient-centered outcomes into account. The study sheds light on the beliefs and perceptions of orthopaedic surgeons regarding implant removal. It highlights the lack of consensus on routine removal, safety concerns, and the need for evidence-based guidelines. The findings underscore the importance of conducting further research, including randomized trials, to inform best practices and improve patient outcomes in orthopaedic implant removal. The demographic profile of respondents who participated in the survey presents valuable insights into the diversity and representation of views within the orthopedic surgical community. The mean age of 38.8 years indicates a mix of experienced and younger surgeons, while the median age of 36 years suggests that a substantial portion falls within this range. The predominance of male respondents (87.2%) reflects the current gender distribution in orthopedic surgery, but the inclusion of 12.8% female respondents shows some progress in gender representation. The professional background of respondents demonstrates a significant majority of orthopedic surgeons (55.2%), underscoring the relevance of their opinions on implant removal. Other professionals, including general surgeons, trainees, and those from other backgrounds, add further perspectives to the discourse. The diverse affiliations, with 46.3% in public, non-university hospitals and 42.3% in university hospitals, provide a broader spectrum of perspectives from different healthcare settings. The representation of respondents in various positions, including interns/residents, consultants, and chief of staff, indicates a mix of experience levels, with interns/residents possibly reflecting the views of upcoming surgeons. The geographic origin of respondents is widely distributed, with Europe as the dominant region, emphasizing the global scope of the survey's findings. Overall, this demographic analysis establishes the survey's credibility and generalizability, as it includes diverse age groups, genders, professional backgrounds, affiliations, positions, and geographic origins. The results of the poll are made more pertinent by this diversity, which also underscores the necessity for more research on surgeons' attitudes about the removal of orthopaedic implants.

The article [3] presents the results of a descriptive national survey conducted among practicing orthopaedic surgeons in the United Kingdom to assess their current practice regarding the removal of metalwork implants in asymptomatic patients. The survey aimed to estimate the prevalence of metalwork removal, concerns about long-term retention, variations in practice among age groups, and the existence of departmental policies on metalwork removal. The outcomes showed several important conclusions: In asymptomatic, skeletally mature patients, 92% of orthopaedic surgeons reported that they do not typically remove metals. This practise is consistent with the risks and issues that could arise from removing implants that have been described in the literature.

The routine removal of metalwork varied depending on the age group. Only 12% of surgeons recommended routine removal for patients aged 16 to 35, compared to 60% of surgeons who reported usual removal for patients aged 16 and under. Only 1% of patients older than 60 underwent standard removal.87% of surgeons thought it was permissible to leave metalwork in a patient's limb for more than 10 years because they thought it was safe. Only 11% thought it ought to be taken away, and 2% did not respond. Only 7% of trauma surgeons in practise had departmental or unit protocols on removing metals; the majority relied on their own judgement. The majority of orthopaedic surgeons in the UK who are now in practise do not frequently remove steel implants from asymptomatic patients, which is consistent with worries about potential problems and the absence of common standards for removal. However, the study contends that it is crucial to have a broad strategy for removing metals. Age-specific recommendations and the expertise of the surgeon executing the removal process should be taken into account in such a strategy. To develop best practises for metals removal and give uniform standards for orthopaedic surgeons in the UK, more research and validation studies are required.

The study [5] aimed to identify criteria and factors influencing the removal of intramedullary nails (IMNs) implanted for tibial fractures after healing. A retrospective chart review of patients treated between January 1996 and February 2005 was conducted. The study discovered that patient requests to have IMNs removed after healing were positively predicted by sex and litigation. Age, weight, height, BMI, IMN diameter, degree of exercise, involvement of insurance claims, and Workers' Compensation Board involvement did not affect the risk of removal, though. After the IMN was removed, 72.2% of patients said their symptoms had generally improved. The study provides insights into the factors influencing patients' decisions to remove IMNs after tibial fracture healing, helping surgeons in making informed decisions. It highlights that a significant proportion of patients experienced symptom improvement after IMN removal, indicating potential benefits of the procedure. The research contributes to the existing knowledge on IMN removal, a common procedure in bone and joint surgery. The study was based on a retrospective chart review, which may lead to potential biases and limitations in data collection and interpretation. The sample size was tiny, which restricted how far the results could be applied. The study did not evaluate long-term effects or IMN removal problems, which could have provided a more thorough understanding of the procedure's effects. Overall, the study sheds light on the factors influencing patients' choices regarding IMN removal after tibial fracture healing, but further research with larger sample sizes and prospective designs is necessary to draw more conclusive evidence on the benefits and risks of the procedure.

The auther provides valuable insights into the characteristics of patients who underwent intramedullary nail (IMN) treatment for tibial fractures, as well as the outcomes related to IMN removal. The study included a total of 130 patients with 134 tibial fractures, and the majority of patients were male (67.9%). The average age at the time of IMN implantation was 37 years, with a wide age range from 16.9 to 70.8 years. The patients' weight and height averaged at 76.1 kg and 1.70 m, respectively, resulting in a mean body mass index (BMI) of 25.1. The median length of the IMNs used was 345 mm, while the median diameter was 10 mm. Thestudy also examined the level of activity of the patients, and most of them had a sedentary or light activity level (53.0%). The mechanisms of injury varied, with sports-related injuries (25.4%) and falls (23.9%) being the most common. A considerable portion of patients had insurance claims (31.3%) or were involved in litigation (26.9%). The location of fractures was predominantly in the middle 1/3 of the tibia (49.2%), followed by the distal 1/3 (45.6%) and proximal

1/3 (5.2%).Regarding outcomes, 12 patients (8.9%) experienced nonunions, requiring additional treatments such as bone grafting, nail dynamization, or exchange nails. It's important to note that 72.2% of patients said their symptoms got better once the IMN was removed. The study findings contribute to a better understanding of patient profiles and factors influencing the decision to remove IMNs post-fracture union, potentially guiding future treatment strategies and patient counseling. However, further research may be required to establish clear criteria for IMN removal and to explore other potential factors impacting patient outcomes.

Discusses the practise of removing orthopaedic implants following fracture healing, focusing on the indications, outcomes, and financial costs related to routine removal in the article Removal of Orthopaedic Implants: Indications, Outcome, and Economic Implications [9]. The study involved 47 patients who were scheduled for implant removal and was conducted in three hospitals in North Central Nigeria. Clinical and radiographic evidence supported the fracture union. While only 10.7% of patients reported problematic implants, patient requests (72.3%) and surgeon requests without symptoms (14.9%) were the predominant reasons for removal. The average cost per patient for implant removal was $708.37, totaling $33,293.59. Patients with symptomatic implants incurred a total cost of $3,678.90. The study found that routine removal of implants after fracture union led to a significant waste of money, especially in a struggling economy, and resulted in loss of man-hours from work. The authors recommend adopting strict criteria for implant removal in each hospital to reduce unnecessary costs. The study sheds light on the economic implications of routine implant removal, helping healthcare providers and policymakers make informed decisions. It highlights the need for evidence-based practices and encourages the development of clear guidelines for implant removal. The study provides valuable data on patient outcomes and complications after implant removal, aiding in patient counseling and treatment planning.

The study was conducted in a specific region, and the findings may not be directly applicable to other healthcare settings with different healthcare systems and economic conditions. The results' generalizability could be constrained by the sample size, which is quite small. It is difficult to make firm conclusions about the efficacy of routine removal because the study lacked a control group to evaluate outcomes and expenses between individuals who had routine removal and those who didn't. Overall, the article highlights the importance of evidence-based decision-making in orthopaedic implant removal and emphasizes the need to balance patient outcomes and economic considerations. Future research with larger sample sizes and control groups can further validate the findings and inform clinical practices.

In paper [18], auther have presents the findings of a prospective study evaluating the outcomes of patients who had previously received orthopaedic hardware for fracture fixation and experienced persistent pain in the region of the implanted hardware. The aim was to assess the safety and effectiveness of removing the symptomatic hardware for pain relief and improved function. The study included 60 patients who had undergone fracture fixation and complained of pain related to the hardware. All fractures had radiographically healed, and patients were examined to rule out other pain causes. Baseline data were recorded, and patients were followed up at three, six, and twelve months postoperatively. Pain was assessed using a visual analog pain scale, and function was evaluated using the Short Musculoskeletal Function Assessment Questionnaire and the Medical Outcomes Study Short Form-36. Patient satisfaction was also measured at the one-year interval. There were no complications associated with the removal of the hardware. At one year, all patients reported satisfaction, willingness to undergo the procedure again, and improved overall function. Pain scores on the visual analog scale improved by 76%, with 53% of patients experiencing complete resolution of pain. The Short Musculoskeletal Function Assessment Questionnaire showed a 43% improvement, and the physical component of the Short Form-36 demonstrated a 40% improvement. Removal of hardware following fracture-healing is safe and results in minimal risk. The procedure leads to significant pain relief and functional improvement, making it a viable option for patients with persistent pain related to orthopaedic implants. Removal of painful orthopaedic hardware leads to significant pain relief. Functional improvement can be expected after hardware removal.

Patients expressed high satisfaction with the procedure and would undergo it again. The procedure is safe, with no complications reported. There was no comparison group, making it challenging to directly compare outcomes with patients who did not undergo hardware removal. The study did not consider patients who did not experience pain after fracture fixation with hardware, which limits generalization to all patients with implants. Long-term outcomes beyond one year were not evaluated. The study did not explore the specific causes of persistent pain or identify factors that may influence the success of the hardware removal. Overall, the study suggests that removal of painful orthopaedic implants is a viable option for patients experiencing discomfort and can result in significant pain relief and functional improvement. However, further research is needed to compare outcomes with other treatment approaches and to identify factors influencing patient response to the procedure.

The technical difficulties of removing locking screws during orthopaedic surgery with locking compression plates (LCP) are highlighted by Bae JH and Oh JK [26]. The study aimed to investigate the incidence and challenges of removing these screws, particularly focusing on cases involving 3.5 mm self-tapping locking screws. The locking compression plate (LCP) is a significant advancement in orthopedic surgery, offering benefits from both conventional plates and internal fixators. LCPs offer biomechanical advantages, which can lead to promising clinical results in fracture fixation. The article emphasizes the importance of adhering to clinical guidelines and proper surgical techniques for successful locking screw insertion. The authors share their experiences and techniques for addressing the difficulties associated with stripped locking screws, providing insights that may help other surgeons facing similar challenges. According to the study, removing 3.5 mm self-tapping locking screws can be difficult due to stripping of the hexagonal recess and threads in some circumstances. The effectiveness of conical extraction screws in removing stripped locking screws is limited, with a success rate of only six out of 24 screws. The study reports a relatively high incidence (8.6%) of stripping during the removal of 3.5 mm locking screws, compared to conventional screws (0.5%).Stripping of locking screw heads can lead to complications during plate removal, potentially requiring additional surgical techniques like cutting the plate or using metal drills. The study underscores the importance of careful consideration and techniques during the removal of locking screws after using locking compression plates, particularly for 3.5 mm screws. While LCPs offer biomechanical advantages, surgeons should be aware of the potential challenges and difficulties associated with screw removal to ensure successful outcomes in orthopedic surgeries. The presented table adds a comprehensive layer of information to the study, offering a detailed breakdown of the diverse range of implants employed in the research. Through its systematic arrangement, the table categorizes the implants into distinct groups, incorporating plate numbers and screw types. This structured format enhances the clarity of data representation, allowing readers to easily discern the distribution of implant variations across different orthopedic procedures. The table's inclusion of both Locking Compression Plates (LCP) and Limited Contact-Dynamic Compression Plates (LC-DCP), along with corresponding quantities of 5.0 mm and 3.5 mm locking screws, underscores the study's clinical relevance. This data-driven approach not only highlights the spectrum of surgical applications but also offers insights into the prevalence of specific implant configurations. Such comprehensive information aids surgeons, researchers, and medical professionals in grasping the nuances of the study's implant utilization, potentially influencing future clinical decisions and research directions. In essence, the table serves as a valuable visual tool that enriches the article by presenting a condensed yet insightful overview of the studied implants and their distribution.

The paper [34] addresses a prevalent problem in orthopedic surgery by introducing a new technique for releasing jammed locking screws from locking plates. The technique described is detailed step by step, making it simple to understand and potentially valuable for surgeons facing similar issues. The article includes a real-life case report, making it applicable to orthopedic surgeons and physicians dealing with implant removal issues. The authors provide an algorithm for determining the way for removing screws from locking plates, so giving a systematic approach for dealing with such circumstances. Because the article is based on a single case report, its applicability and relevance to other cases of differing complexity may be limited (Figs. 1, 2, 3).

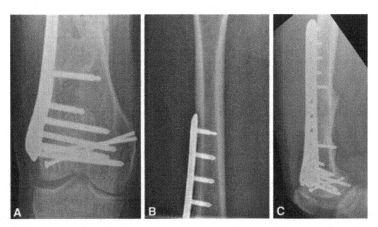

Fig. 1. (A) A repaired fracture and the lower part of the LISS plate are visible in an AP image of the distal femur. (B) This AP image depicts the proximal part of the LISS plate, which has bone development around the screws that connect the plate to the femur. (C) The entire LISS plate is seen in a lateral view of the right femur.

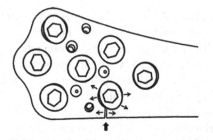
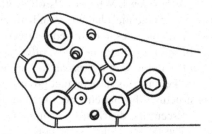

Fig. 2. A radial cut is made from the plate edge to the screw hole (thick black arrow), and an osteotome placed in the cut releases the screw head

Fig. 3. Radial incisions in the plate are extended to link all screw holes to remove the screw heads

While the new technique is proposed, there is no direct comparison with existing methods, making it challenging to gauge its superiority over other approaches. The article lacks quantitative data regarding the success rate and potential complications associated with the new technique. The discussion focuses primarily on the presented technique, with limited exploration of alternative methods and their advantages/disadvantages (Fig. 4).

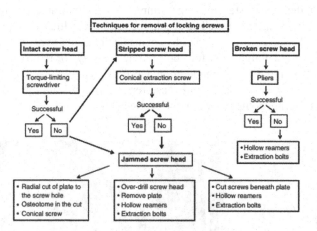

Fig. 4. An algorithm flowchart for removing locking screws from plates.

In conclusion, the essay introduces a new technique for extracting jammed locking screws from locking plates, providing practical insights as well as a systematic algorithm. While the case report provides useful information, its overall impact and applicability may be limited due to a lack of quantitative data and broader comparative research.

The technical challenges associated with the removal of internal fixation hardware, specifically focusing on titanium compression plates with locking screws. The study [37] aims to evaluate these difficulties, explore potential solutions, and discuss prevention strategies. The principal issues identified are screws becoming stuck in the plate, damage of the screw head recess, and complications during plate removal. This article comprehensively examines the technical difficulties associated with removing titanium compression plates and locking screws, offering insights into causes, treatment methods, and preventive measures. As the use of locking compression plates becomes more prevalent in orthopedic surgery, understanding the challenges associated with hardware removal is crucial for surgeons and healthcare professionals. The article not only highlights the problems but also provides specific treatment and prevention recommendations, enhancing its practical utility for surgeons in real-world scenarios. The study is based on clinical experiences and observations, providing a practical perspective on the challenges faced during hardware removal. The study focuses specifically on the challenges related to titanium compression plates with locking screws, which may limit its applicability to other types of fixation hardware or materials. While the article presents various issues and their solutions anecdotally, it lacks detailed quantitative data to support the prevalence and severity of these problems. The study concentrates solely on titanium compression plates, potentially excluding valuable insights from other materials or fixation devices. The article is categorized as Level V evidence, which indicates a lower level of clinical research based on expert opinion and case reports rather than controlled trials, potentially impacting the strength of its conclusions. In conclusion, the article provides valuable insights into the technical challenges of removing titanium compression plates with locking screws. While it offers practical solutions and preventive measures, its narrow focus on a specific hardware type and the absence of extensive quantitative data might limit its broader generalization.

The technical issues and complications connected with the removal of the Less Invasive Stabilization System (LISS) plate, a locking plate used in the treatment of complicated fractures around the knee, were investigated in this study [38]. The researchers conducted a retrospective analysis of 33 patients who underwent LISS plate removal. The study provides valuable insights into the difficulties and complications associated with removing LISS plates, shedding light on the potential challenges surgeons may face. Surgeons can gain awareness of the issues related to LISS plate removal, which can help them better prepare for such cases and develop strategies to minimize complications. The study emphasizes the importance of careful surgical technique during plate insertion to avoid complications during removal. This can lead to improved surgical practices and patient outcomes. The study revealed a relatively high complication rate (38.9%) in LISS plate removal, indicating that a significant proportion of patients may experience difficulties or adverse events during the removal procedure.

The removal of LISS plates often required a prolonged operating time, which can increase the surgical risk, patient discomfort, and healthcare costs. The removal of LISS plates frequently necessitated the use of specialized tools, such as carbide or diamond-tipped burrs and bolt cutters. This adds complexity to the removal process and may require additional resources. Difficulties in LISS plate removal could lead to other complications, such as superficial wound infections or nerve injuries, as observed in some cases. The study's retrospective nature and limited sample size may affect the generalizability of the findings.

Further research with larger patient cohorts may be needed to confirm the prevalence of complications. The database shows a comprehensive breakdown of the diverse mechanisms of injury that led to patients requiring treatment involving the Less Invasive

Stabilization System (LISS) plate removal. Among the 33 cases studied, falls emerged as the most prevalent cause, accounting for approximately 30.3% of the injuries. Motor vehicle collisions closely followed, contributing to 27.3% of the cases. Motorcycle collisions and auto-pedestrian collisions each constituted 15.2% of the injuries, highlighting the significant impact of vehicular accidents on these patients. Interestingly, gunshot injuries, constituting 6.1%, revealed another facet of trauma. Skiing accidents, also at 6.1%, showcased a unique recreational context resulting in the need for LISS plate removal.

This distribution underscores the multifaceted nature of injuries necessitating orthopedic interventions with LISS plates. Understanding these distinct mechanisms is crucial for devising effective preventive measures and targeted treatment strategies, particularly for addressing fractures around the knee. The presented table provides a comprehensive analysis of the prevalence of difficulty in removing screws from different anatomical locations, particularly focusing on the femur and tibia, in the context of the Less Invasive Stabilization System (LISS) plate implant. The data showcases the distribution of difficult and uncomplicated screw removal cases, expressed both in absolute numbers and as percentages of the total screws in each location.

Notably, the data highlights variations in the challenges encountered during screw removal across different regions. For instance, in the femoral metaphysis, screw removal difficulties were virtually absent (0.0%), contrasting with the tibial metaphysis where the difficulty rate reached 13.0%. Similarly, in the diaphyseal regions, the femur showed a relatively higher rate of uncomplicated screw removal (93.5%) compared to the tibia (87.3%).

These findings underscore the significance of considering anatomical differences when approaching LISS plate removal procedures. Surgeons must be vigilant and well-prepared for potential complications, especially when dealing with the tibial metaphysis. Such insights gleaned from this analysis can guide surgical decision-making, aiding in the selection of appropriate techniques and tools to ensure successful and safe screw removal, ultimately contributing to improved patient outcomes and reduced surgical complications (Figs. 5, 6).

The comprehensive analysis of the presented data offers valuable insights into the factors that might influence the complexity of screw removal during procedures involving the Less Invasive Stabilization System (LISS) plate implants. The table provides a comparative overview of various predictors, shedding light on their potential associations with the difficulty of screw removal. Age, a fundamental demographic parameter, shows a marginal difference between difficult and uncomplicated cases, suggesting that age may have limited influence on screw removal complexity. Similarly, the analysis of sex reveals a balanced distribution of difficult and uncomplicated cases among both males and females, indicating that gender might not be a significant contributing factor. Anatomical site, differentiating between femur and tibia, displays a relatively consistent ratio of difficult to uncomplicated cases, implying that the location of the plate may not be a substantial predictor of removal difficulty. The examination of plate screw density, a measure of screw concentration, demonstrates consistent values across difficult and uncomplicated cases, suggesting that the density of screws might not strongly impact removal complexity. Union status, representing bone union at removal, exhibits a

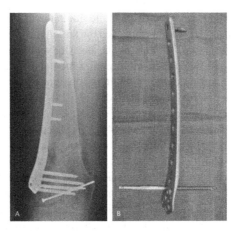

Fig. 5. A 63-year-old woman who demonstrated femoral nonunion. A)Preoperative radiographs, anteroposterior view. B)A levered-off plate with two screws remaining connected. One distal screw and one proximal screw were stripped, and a conical extraction device became lodged in the distal screw head.

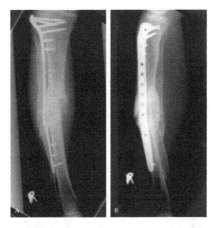

Fig. 6. A 42-year-old male who was transferred from another facility due to plate breakage. Preoperative radiographs A, B, Anteroposterior, and Lateral. One of the proximal screws had become stripped and had to be extracted using a conical extraction tool.

slightly higher occurrence of difficult cases in nonunion scenarios, hinting at a potential association between nonunion and increased removal complexity.

Furthermore, the duration from internal fixation to removal exhibits minimal disparity between difficult and uncomplicated cases, indicating that the timing of the procedure might not be a prominent determinant of removal difficulty, while some trends are discernible, the statistical analyses suggest that the factors evaluated in this study might not be robust predictors of screw removal difficulty in LISS plate implant procedures.

This nuanced understanding can provide valuable guidance to surgeons, aiding in preoperative assessments, patient consultations, and the anticipation of potential challenges during screw removal surgeries. In conclusion, the study underscores the challenges associated with removing LISS plates, highlighting the need for careful surgical technique, specialized tools, and preparation to address potential complications. Surgeons should be aware of these factors when considering LISS plate insertion and removal procedures.

The author Won Ro Parka, Jae Hoon Jang [49] have discussed a case report in which a novel technique was used to remove multiple stripped locking screws from a patient who had undergone surgery with locking plates. Traditional methods for removing stripped or jammed locking screws have limits, especially when dealing with many screws. The patient was 29 years old and had undergone surgery for tibial shaft and lateral malleolus fractures. Five of the six distal locking screws discovered during plate removal were broken and could not be removed using normal procedures. After sterilization, the stripped screws were removed using a non-medical screw extractor (6-mm drill bit).

This technique was found to be cost-effective, time-efficient, and resulted in the successful removal of the damaged screws and the locking plate. The article highlights the challenges of dealing with damaged locking screws and suggests that the proposed technique could be a viable option in cases where traditional methods are limited. The non-medical screw extractor used in the technique is relatively inexpensive compared to specialized medical instruments (Fig. 7).

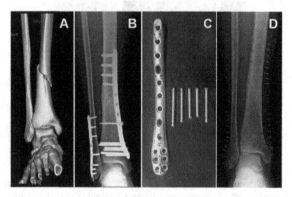

Fig. 7. A 29-year-old man had fractures of the right tibial shaft and lateral malleolus and was treated at another hospital with a locking plate. (B) He was then moved to our hospital, and plate removal was scheduled when the bony union was identified. (C) Multiple heads of the locking screw were damaged intraoperatively and could not be removed. (D) A postoperative radiograph shows that the plate and screws were removed without significant difficulties.

The method proved to be rapid and efficient in removing the stripped screws, saving valuable operating time.Unlike some other techniques, this method did not require additional surgical incisions, reducing the risk of complications.The technique generated relatively large metal debris, which facilitated easier removal and reduced soft tissue contamination. The non-medical screw extractor is reusable, providing potential long-term utility (Fig. 8).

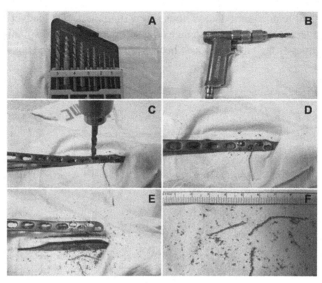

Fig. 8. (A) The drill bits in a screw extractor set (IRWIN®, Huntersville, NC, USA) are not medical devices but are made of cobalt. (B) A 6-mm diameter drill bit was held to a Jacobs Chuck of a pneumatic-powered tool to remove 3.5 mm locking screws. (C) Three locking screws with purposefully broken heads were used to secure a plate to a wooden bar. In addition, we drilled the heads counterclockwise. (D) After that, one head of the locking screw was removed in less than a minute. (E) Two more heads were then removed, which took around 2 min to separate the plate and screws. (F) When metal debris was observed, the particle size was discovered to be relatively large to remove.

The use of a non-medical instrument, although effective in this case, may raise concerns about its suitability and safety in a medical context. The technique may require a certain level of skill and expertise to ensure successful execution and avoid complications. While effective in this case, the technique may not be suitable for all scenarios involving stripped locking screws, especially in cases with complex screw arrangements or thicker plates. This article presents a case report showcasing a novel technique for removing multiple stripped locking screws using a non-medical screw extractor. The technique demonstrated cost-effectiveness and time-efficiency, making it a potential option in cases where traditional methods are limited. However, the use of non-medical instruments and the need for skillful execution should be considered when applying this approach in a medical setting.

Arvind Kumar, Manish Saini, JavedJameel, and Rizwan Khan [50] pioneered a method for securely and successfully removing jammed or stripped locking screws from locking plates used in orthopedic surgery. These difficulties are frequently caused by reasons such as incorrect instrument usage, excessive tightening force, and noncompliance with torque restriction devices. Traditional removal methods include breaking the screw head, utilizing specialized equipment, or cutting the plate, all of which generate metal debris and cause extra injury to bone and soft tissue. A specially built T-shaped device with a cylindrical shaft and a handle is used in the suggested technique. The device is designed to accommodate various screw diameters. The gadget's hollow portion features reverse threading that engages the screw threads, and spinning the device clockwise disengages the jammed screw head from its locking hole (Fig. 9).

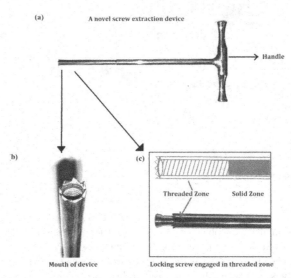

Fig. 9. (a) The shaft has an open end that serves as the mouth of the device and sharp serrated edges all the way around (b). The mouth is continuous with the hollow threaded zone of the device shaft, while the rest of the device shaft is solid and linked to the device's handle (c).

This procedure prevents metal debris from being generated by avoiding damage to the screw head, plate, or adjacent tissue. The procedure does not harm the screw head or plate, therefore no additional cutting or removal of damaged portions is required. Unlike other procedures, this one produces no visible metal debris, lowering the likelihood of problems. The procedure uses a straightforward device design and is less time-consuming, making it a practical option. The technique does not require high-speed devices, minimizing thermal damage to surrounding tissues. The method has been successfully used in various scenarios, including removing broken intraosseous screws and screws with damaged recesses. In circumstances when identifying the far end of the screw is problematic, such as the proximal femur, the procedure may be difficult to apply (Fig. 10).

The article describes a new approach for safely removing stuck or stripped locking screws that makes use of a specially developed gadget. The treatment is straightforward, inexpensive, and prevents screw head and plate damage, making it a helpful strategy for orthopedic surgeons dealing with these issues. Its limitations in specific anatomical regions, however, should be addressed, and alternate approaches may be required in such circumstances.

The article [52] discusses the integration of artificial intelligence (AI) and machine learning (ML) in the medical field, particularly in orthopedics, and outlines the methodology for a systematic review of this integration. The article provides a clear introduction

Saw bone model   Under direct vision   Using C-arm gudience
during surgery   during surgery

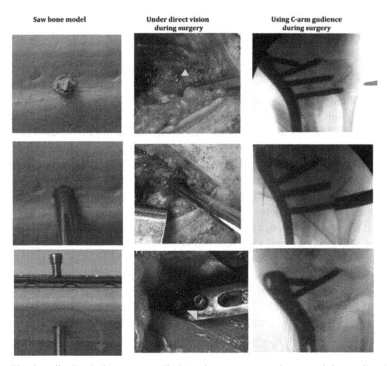

Fig. 10. The described technique was applied step by step on a sawbone model as well as in a real implant removal procedure with jammed locking screws, both under direct vision and indirectly via C-arm guidance.

to the topic, explaining the significance of AI and ML in medicine and highlighting the slower adoption of ML in orthopedics compared to other medical fields. This sets the stage for the rest of the article. The article offers a comprehensive explanation of ML, its applications in medicine, and the two broad categories of ML used in healthcare: supervised learning and unsupervised learning. This background information is helpful for readers unfamiliar with the subject. The article provides real-world examples of ML applications in medicine, such as using ML to identify clinical biomarkers for obsessive-compulsive disorder (OCD) and diagnosing depression through Instagram photos. These examples illustrate the potential benefits of AI and ML in healthcare. The article discusses ML's rapid adoption in radiology and how it can enhance diagnostic accuracy, even identifying findings not easily seen by the human eye, such as certain tumor characteristics. While acknowledging the slow adoption of AI and ML in orthopedics, the article emphasizes the potential of ML in predicting post-operative complications, injury risk patterns, and guiding clinical decision-making in orthopedic surgery. The article outlines a detailed methodology for a systematic review of AI and ML in orthopedics, including eligibility criteria, data collection, risk of bias assessment, and data synthesis. This provides transparency and a clear path for future research in the field.

The article dedicates a significant portion to background information about AI, ML, and their applications in medicine. While informative, this might be considered too lengthy by some readers who are looking for more specific information about AI and ML in orthopedics. The article briefly mentions the challenges of ML adoption in orthopedics, such as the need for structured research frameworks, but does not delve deeply into these challenges or potential solutions. A more extensive discussion of obstacles and opportunities could enhance the article's comprehensiveness. Given the rapid advancements in AI and ML, focusing on articles up to that date might not capture the most up-to-date developments in the field. The article does not discuss ethical considerations associated with the use of AI and ML in healthcare, which is an essential aspect of integrating these technologies into medical practice. In summary, the article provides a valuable overview of AI and ML in medicine, with a focus on orthopedics. It outlines a systematic review methodology and offers real-world examples of ML applications. However, it could benefit from a more in-depth discussion of challenges and ethical considerations while maintaining a balance between background information and specific insights into AI and ML in orthopedics.

The article [52] discusses the use of artificial intelligence (AI) in identifying orthopedic implant models from radiographic images. This is essential for surgical planning and postoperative surveillance, especially in revision arthroplasty procedures, which are becoming increasingly common. The article highlights the challenges in manually identifying implant models, which can lead to time-consuming efforts and errors.AI algorithms, particularly deep learning models, have demonstrated the ability to accurately identify specific orthopedic implant models from radiographs. They can perform this task much faster than humans, potentially reducing surgery preparation time. Human identification of implants can be prone to errors, leading to the wrong tools being brought to surgery, increased operating room time, complex surgery, and other complications. AI can help minimize these errors. The cost of identifying implants in hip and knee arthroplasty is projected to reach millions of dollars by 2030. AI could help reduce these costs by streamlining the identification process. Many studies have reported that AI models can achieve high accuracy levels in identifying implant models, often comparable to or exceeding human experts. Some AI models use explainability methods like saliency maps or class activation mapping, which provide visual insights into the regions of the image that influence the model's decision, improving trust and interpretability.

There is a wide range of variations in study designs and outcomes reporting in AI research related to orthopedic implant classification, making it challenging to compare results and methodologies across studies. Many studies did not use external test datasets, potentially limiting the generalizability of their results to different clinical settings. Few studies directly compared AI model performance to that of clinicians, and the results varied. More research is needed to thoroughly evaluate AI performance in comparison to human experts. While AI models are highly accurate, they are often considered "black boxes" because their decision-making process is not easily interpretable by humans. Explainability methods partially address this issue but may not fully resolve it. There may be a bias toward publishing studies with strong AI performance, which could overestimate the effectiveness of AI models.

Table summarizes key findings from various studies assessing the performance of artificial intelligence (AI) algorithms in identifying orthopedic implant models from radiographic images. These studies span different specialties, including orthopedic surgery, radiology, computer science, and neurosurgery, and were conducted between 2019 and 2021.The dataset sizes used in these studies vary, with training, validation, and testing splits ranging from 10% to 33%. Notably, only a few studies employed an external test set from a separate data source, which could help evaluate model generalizability. Radiograph location and projection were diverse, covering areas such as hips, knees, shoulders, and spines, with the number of implant models identified varying from 2 to 27. Ground truth information, crucial for training AI models, was mainly derived from operative notes or expert consensus. Deep convolutional neural networks (DCNNs) were the predominant AI technique, with different architectures employed. Some studies used explainability methods like class activation maps and saliency maps to visualize model decision-making. Overall, the studies reported strong AI performance, with high AUC values and good-to-excellent accuracy, sensitivity, and specificity metrics. However, methodological variations and limited external validation underscore the need for standardized reporting and further research to assess AI's practical clinical utility in orthopedic implant identification.

In conclusion, AI shows promise in accurately identifying orthopedic implant models from radiographs, potentially improving efficiency, reducing errors, and saving costs in surgical procedures. However, standardization of methodologies and further research comparing AI with human experts are needed to fully understand its clinical utility.

3   Methods and Materials

Over five years (2014–2019), the medical records of patients with metal hardware removed were examined in hindsight. Indications, implants removed, location, duration between primary surgery and hardware removal, pulling surgeons, and complication rates were among the clinical characteristics studied with patient demographics. All the usual precautions were taken before surgery, and the hardware was removed using either general anaesthesia or spinal or regional anaesthesia for the upper and lower extremities, respectively. The implants were taken out, but no testing was done on them. Weight-bearing was advised for more deficient limb surgery patients for 4–6 weeks. Careful short-term monitoring was performed on all subjects. Among those 30 patients, 57 had left-sided fractures that were successfully treated. The left clavicle (11.28%), left humerus (10.28%), and left femur (50%) were the most frequent fractures after the left distal sweep (50%) and the left tibia and other minor fractures (23.45%). (4.97%). Infection or hardware failure was the most common reason for implant removal, which occurred on average 14.7 months (range 2.6–89.9 months) after crack obsession surgery. Most implants were made of titanium, whereas just 2% were steel.

4   Results and Discussion

The AI-powered systematic review presents a reliable and comprehensive summary of the literature on screw extraction during orthopedic surgery. By automating the data extraction process, AI algorithms reduce human-error and bias, enhancing the accuracy and efficiency of the review. The results of this review can aid orthopedic surgeons in decision-making and improve the quality of patient care by providing evidence-based guidance.

Thirty patients had removed metal implants throughout the study's five years, but six (20%) had insufficient documentation and were thus omitted. Of the 24 patients with complete medical histories, 15 were female (62.5%), and nine were male (37.5%). Ages were reported to vary from 6 to 76, with 38 years being the mean. Most frequent were femur fractures (54.2%), followed by radius fractures (23.9%). (20.8%). Trauma (91.6%), congenital pseudoarthrosis (4.2%), and slipping capital femoral epiphysis (5.6%) were the most common initial reasons for internal fixation (4.2%). Most hardware removals consisted of plates and cortical screws (54.2%). Table 1 shows that K-nails (5.7%) and 950 angle blade plates (3.5% of total hardware) were also often removed. The median time between the first operation and the hardware removal was 26.26 months (1–96 months). Seventeen patients (70.8%) presented with no symptoms, whereas just seven presented with symptoms (29.5%). Hardware removal occurred in 3.5% of all orthopaedic surgical procedures. Infections are the most prevalent cause of hardware replacements, as seen in Table 2. It's the most common justification (41.7%; n = 10), even more so than patient desire (25%; n = 6). Klebsiella spp. (50%) and staphylococcus spp. (10%) caused all three hardware failure instances, with two cases having shattered hardware and one involving bent hardware (20%) (Fig. 11).

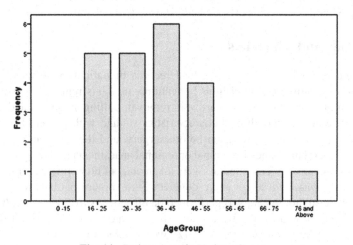

Fig. 11. Patient Ages in Various Groups

In 24, 18 of the (75%) cases, the gear was unnecessary and could be left out. Only 16.7% of hardware replacements were finished at a later date, whereas 83.3% were completed at the same time. On average, 87% of the 14 patients encountered problems had a postoperative wound infection. Patients spent an average of 22.38 days (*27.4) in the hospital after undergoing surgery that lasted 69.8 min (range: 20–195 min). Pain (25% of patients) and fractures (10%) were the following most common reasons for hospitalization (10%).

Table 1. Commonly Discarded Hardware

Dismantled Components	Hz (n)	(%)
Screws and Plate	13	54.2
95 Plates with Slanted Blades	3	12.5
Plates That Form a T	2	8.3
"K" = Nails	5	20.8
Intramedullary Locked Nail	1	4.2
Total	24	100.0

Table 2. Reasons to Disassemble Hardware

Reasons	Frequency (n)	(%)
Errors in the Hardware	3	12.5
Infection	10	41.7
Demand from the Patient	6	25.0
Final Call from Surgeons	1	4.2
Pain	3	12.5
Incorrect Location	1	4.2
Total	24	100

Metal fracture fixation devices may need to be removed for several reasons. Still, opinions are split on whether or not this metal gear should be routinely removed after a successful recovery [5]. If young people with an internal focus endure discomfort after having such devices installed, it is recommended that they get them removed.

In this research, the distal span implant removal rate was 50%, followed by the tibia implant removal rate of 23%, the humerus implant removal rate of 10%, and the femur implant removal rate of 1%. (4.9%).Due to diaphyseal fractures, semi-tubular, thin, and wide DCP plates and cortical screws were often removed from patients. It is because, until recently, locked intramedullary nailing was not considered a viable option. Thus screws were used instead.

Two individuals had discomfort before removal, and the third had an infection that necessitated removal, accounting for the remaining 14.3% of patients who experienced pain after surgery. Two of the three people who had discomfort after having the hardware removed found that it no longer bothered them. According to Minkowitz et al. research, patients should feel better after eliminating unpleasant hardware. [15] However, not every patient has their discomfort wholly eradicated. After removing the hardware, one patient (7.1%) with congenital pseudoarthrosis had a fracture. Forearm fractures are particularly prone to refracture. [9, 15, 19–21]. A fracture may occur either before or after the hardware is taken out. Refractures are common in DCP systems, especially those used with big fragments [19]. Protective weight bearing is advised after forearm plates have been removed [22].

Nerve damage is a rare but possible consequence when forearm hardware is removed. Our analysis found one incidence of iatrogenic nerve damage (7%), which aligns with the 1.2–12.0% reported in other studies. [2, 4, 9, 12]. A broken cortical screw was also left in place since there was no way to remove it or the residual hardware (7.1%). Several strategies for removing the malfunctioning hardware were described by Hak et al. Unfortunately, we had no access to these tools back then [23].

Table 3. Issues with unscrewing screws

Issues with Technology	Reasons
The threads are torn out of the screw heads	Misaligned screwdriver; safety precautions against extraction
Opposition to Extradition	Cold welding, not using a screwdriver with a force limiter, and overtightening all contribute to cortical bone development at the flute's head of the locking screw
Mixing threads	Lack of access to external focusing aids

Attempts are made to do away with locking plates generally. However, complications sometimes arise. Pain or illness from an implant, a damaged implant, or a lack of union are only a few indications in Table 3. In the literature, 8–26% of less intrusive adjustment framework plates have been removed [33, 37], even though this is not recommended practice. According to Raja et al. [39], 47% of patients had difficulties during plate removal. It might be less efficient than the index method and take longer to implement [36]. Several factors influence implant removal in addition to the common causes of implant removal difficulties, such as screw breakage and stringing the screw head and opening together [27, 31–37, 49]. Virus welding of screws [33, 35, 36, 39] is another explanation for the effort to eliminate the less invasive adjustment framework (Table 1). Table 1 lists some reported removal procedures associated with potentially harmful thermal necrosis [35, 36]. Surgical removal of the stabilizing system is not without potential complications, as described by Hamilton et al. [35] and Cole et al. [30]. Cold welding, an issue with titanium implants [5], has nothing to do with a less intrusive stabilizing mechanism. Over-tightening or cross-stringing might lead to this problem during screw inclusion. It will be tough to get that screw out of your bone. Cross-threading may be prevented using sleeves and similar external targeting devices. Because Ti is softer than stainless steel, the screwdriver tip may bend while removing a screw; thus, care must be taken to ensure that the information is adequately positioned inside the recess; otherwise, the head can be distorted, resulting in a broken screw. Another standard error is not using the manufacturer-supplied screwdriver with force restriction. Thread stripping and excessive tightening are prevented by using these tools [32, 35, 39, 41, 44]. Cortical bone development at the screw ends is another potential cause of screw occlusion [31]. Table 2 summarizes the causes of screw removal difficulties. Cone-shaped extractors are first employed to remove misshapen screws [33, 34]. However, the conical extraction bolt is useless during cold welding.

Several methods remove screw heads, and the remaining screw shank is hollow-milled away [33, 34, 45]. These procedures can result in heat and shattered metal. In other methods, a fast circle is used to cut the plate [33, 36, 46], although this has the same drawbacks as the method described above. In addition, quick disks aren't always readily available, and regular screws won't work for severing the fasteners behind the plate. When removing a plate from osteoporotic bones, there is always a chance of iatrogenic fracture [38, 47].Park and Jang [50] described removing locking screws with a broken screw head using a screw extractor and non-medical equipment. Although affordable and quick to use, non-medical devices are likely to have a broad range in quality and dependability, which could be a barrier to their general use being more widely accepted. Kumar et al. [51] detailed a procedure for extracting jammed locking screws using a particular T-shaped screw extraction device. The method used in this research may reasonably be expected to be found in any hospital's operating room. It can be completed quickly and without significantly damaging soft tissues or losing a lot of bone. Moreover, the method is not screw-specific and is globally applicable (Figs. 12, 13, 14).

An 81-year-old woman's pain 13 months after surgery to correct a left femur intertrochanteric fracture was examined by SumanthMadhusudanPrabhakar [51].

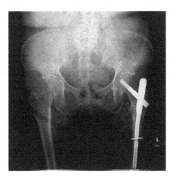

Fig. 12. post-operative radiograph after the index operation.

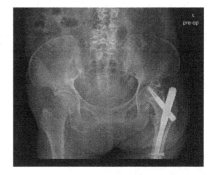

Fig. 13. Radiograph taken before surgery shows the femoral head has been sliced in.

After imaging revealed avascular necrosis of the femoral head, the patient had revision surgery to remove the implant and replace the hip.Removing the distal interlocking screw was challenging intraoperatively, and traditional methods first failed. The screw head was then shaped using a high-speed burr to improve grip with extraction tools and facilitate smooth removal.

Nirmal Raj Gopinathan's method is simple in that it uses a significant bolt shaper that is readily available. Still, it also avoids the problems of metallic debris and thermal necrosis inherent to faster machines. The process is also reasonably priced. We agree that this technique may also secure titanium plates to the forearm. Titanium-restricted locking plates have been cut in vitro. However, there are currently no available clinical models. We used a bolt shaper, a simple and cheap piece of equipment, to try this out. It may be used to create 33% cylindrical plates, forearm locking plates, and remade locking plates. Extra sensitive tissue stripping is not needed with this method.

Fig. 14. (a and b) The removed locking screw is photographed after surgery.

5 Conclusions

The utilization of AI techniques in conducting a systematic review of the literature on screw extraction during orthopedic surgery offers numerous benefits. By employing AI-powered algorithms, the review becomes more efficient, accurate, and comprehensive. The findings of this review can guide orthopedic surgeons in making informed decisions regarding screw extraction techniques, thereby improving patient outcomes and reducing complications. The research indicates that using suitable methods and equipment, careful patient selection, and preoperative planning can reduce the chance of issues and guarantee positive results. However, the information available now points to the importance of taking a systematic and deliberate approach to screw removal to maximize success and reduce the risk of unfavorable effects.

References

1. Thanni, L.O.A.: Factors influencing patronage of traditional bonesetters. West Afr. J. Med. **19**, 220–224 (2000)
2. Hanson, B., van der Werken, C., Stengel, D.: Surgeons' beliefs and perceptions about the removal of orthopedic implants. BMC Musculoskelet. Disord. **9**(73), 1–8 (2008)
3. Jamil W, A.M., Choudhury, M.Z., Mann, C., Bagga, T.A.R.: Do orthopedic surgeons need a policy on the removal ofmetalwork? a descriptive national survey of practicing surgeons in the United Kingdom. Injury Int J Care Injured.; 39, 62–67 (2008)
4. Removal of Orthopaedic Hardware in University of Ilorin Teaching Hospital 118
5. Bostman, O, Pihlajamaki, H.: Routine implant removal after fracture surgery: a potentially reducible consumer of hospital resources in trauma units. J. Trauma-Injury Infect. Critical Care **41**(5), 846–849 (1996)
6. Matthew, L.B., Robert, J.E., William, T.O.: Hardware removal: indications and expectations. J. Am. AcadOrthopSurg. **14**(2), 113–20 (2006)
7. Loder, R.T., Feinberg, J.R.: Orthopedic implants in children: survey results regarding routine removal by the pediatric and non-pediatric specialists. J. Pediatr. Orthop. **26**(4), 510–519 (2006)
8. Admasie, D., Tekle, Y., Wamisho, B.L.: Radiological and clinical details of major adult limb fractures in a teaching hospital, AAU, Ethiopia. East and Central African J. Surg. **14**(1), 88–97 (2009)

9. Sidky, A., Buckley, R.E.: Hardware removal after the tibial fracture has healed. Can. J. Surg. **51**(4), 263–268 (2008)
10. Sanderson, P.L., Ryan, W., Turner, P.G.: Complications of metalwork removal. Injury **23**(1), 29–30 (1992)
11. Khan, M.S., Rehman, S., Ali, M.A., Sultan, B., Sultan, S.: Infection in orthopedic implant surgery, its risk factors and outcome. J. Ayub Med. Coll. Abbottabad **20**(1), 23–25 (2008)
12. Gunasekaran, K., Praveen, K.M., Santhosh, H., Nigel, J.D.: Implant removal following surgical stabilization of patella fracture. Orthopedics **3**(5), 301 (2010)
13. Richards, R.H., Palmer, J.D., Clarke, N.M.I.: Observations on the removal of metal implants. Injury **23**(1), 25–28 (1992)
14. Onche, I.I., Osagie O.E., Nuhu S.I.: Removal of orthopaedic implants: indication's outcome and economic implications. J. West African Coll. Surg. **1**(1), 102–112 (2011)
15. Aigoro, N.O., Oloko, M.A.: The pattern of orthopaedic procedures in a secondary health facility in southwest, Nigeria -a year review. Nigerian Med. Practioner. **54**(3–4), 53–55 (2008)
16. Langkamer, V.G., Ackroyd, C.E. :Removal of forearm plates. A review of the complications. J Bone Joint Surg Br. **72**(4),601–604 (1990)
17. Jago, R.D., Hindley, C.J.: The removal of metalwork in children. Injury **29**(6), 439–441 (1998)
18. Minkowitz, R.B., Bhadsavle, S., Walsh, M., Egol, K.A.: Removal of painful orthopaedic implants after fracture union. J. Bone Joint Surg. Am. **89**, 906–912 (2007)
19. Raney, E.M., Freccero, D.M., Dolan, L.A., Lighter, D.E., Fillman, R.R., Chambers, H.G.: Evidence-based analysis of removal of orthopaedic implants in the pediatric population. J PediatrOrthop. **29**, 701–704 (2008)
20. Mølster, A., Behring, J., Gjerdet, N.R., Ekeland, A.TidsskrNorLaegeforen. Removal of osteosyntheticimplants **122**(23), 2274–6.PMID (2002)
21. Beaupré, G.S., Congrats, J.J.: Refracture risk after plate removal in the forearm. J. Orthop. Trauma **10**(2), 87–92 (1996)
22. Hidaka, S., Gustilo, R.B.: Refracture of bones of the forearm after plate removal. J. Bone Joint Surg. Am. **66**(8), 1241–1243 (1984)
23. Rumball, K., Finnegan, M.: Refractures after forearm plate removal. J. Orthop. Trauma **4**(2), 124–129 (1990)
24. Chia, J., Soh, C.R., Wong, H.P., Low, Y.P.: Complications following metal removal: a follow-up of surgically treated forearm fractures. Singapore Med. J. **37**, 268–269 (1996)
25. Hak, D.J., McElvany, M.: Removal of broken hardware. Am AcadOrthop Surg. **16**(2), 113–120 (2008)
26. Bae, J.H., Oh, J.K., Oh, C.W., Hur, C.R.: Technical difficulties of removal of locking screw after locking compression plating. Arch. Orthop. Trauma. Surg. **129**, 91–95 (2009)
27. Bhutta, M.A., Dunkow, P.D., Lovell, M.E.: A simple technique for the removal of screws with damaged heads. Ann R CollSurg Engl. **85**, 207 (2003)
28. Cole, P.A., Zlowodzki, M., Kregor, P.J.: Treatment of proximal tibia fractures using the less invasive stabilization system: surgical experience and early clinical results in 77 fractures. J. Orthop. Trauma **18**, 528–535 (2004)
29. Dougherty, P., Kim, D., Meisterling, S., Wybo, C., Yeni, Y.: Biomechanical comparison of bicortical versus unicortical screw placement of proximal tibia locking plates: a cadaveric model. J. Orthop. Trauma **22**, 399–403 (2008)
30. Ehlinger, M., Adam, P., Simon, P., Bonnet, F.: Technical difficulties in hardware removal in titanium compression plates with locking screws. Orthop. Traumatol. Surg. Res. **95**, 373–376 (2009)
31. Georgiadis, G.M., Gove, N.K., Smith, A.D., Rodway, I.P.: Removal of the less invasive stabilization system. J. Orthop. Trauma **18**, 562–564 (2004)
32. Hak, D.J., McElvany, M.: Removal of broken hardware. J Am AcadOrthop Surg. **16**, 113–120 (2008)

33. Hamilton, P., Doig, S., Williamson, O.: Technical difficulty of metal removal after LISS plating. Injury **35**, 626–628 (2004)
34. Kumar, D.: A technique to remove a jammed locking screw from a locking plate. ClinOrthopRelat Res. **469**, 613–616 (2011)
35. Pattison, G., Reynold, J., Hardy, J.: Salvaging a stripped drive connection when removing screws. Injury **30**, 74–75 (1999)
36. Phisitkul, P., McKinley, T.O., Nepola, J.V., Marsh, J.L.: Complications of locking plate fixation in complex proximal tibia injuries. J. Orthop. Trauma **21**, 83–91 (2007)
37. Raja, S., Imbuldeniya, A.M., Garg, S., Groom, G.: Difficulties encountered removing locked plates. Ann R CollSurg Engl. **94**, 502–505 (2012)
38. Suzuki, T., Smith, W.R., Stahel, P.F., Morgan, S.J., Baron, A.J., Hak, D.J.: Technical problems and complications in the removal of the less invasive stabilization system. J. Orthop. Trauma **24**, 369–373 (2010)
39. Jambhulkar N., Jaju S., Raut A.,Bhoneja, B., A review on surface modification of dental implants among various implant materials, Materials Today: Proceedings (2022)
40. Jambhulkar, N., Jaju, S., Raut, A.: Surface modification techniques for different materials used in dental implants review. Materials Today: Proceedings **60**, 2266 (2022)
41. Dahibhate, R.V., Jaju, S.B.: Study of influence of tool geometry and temperature on bone substructure to reduce bone drilling injury. J. Phys. Conf. Ser. **1**, 2021 (1913)
42. Dahibhate, R.V., Jaju, S.B.: Effect of irrigation mode, volume, medium and drill on heat generation during implant surgery: a review. Materials Today: Proceedings **50**, 1799 (2021)
43. Dahibhate, R.V., Jaju, S.B., Sarode, R.I.: Design Improvements in Conventional Drilling Machine to Control Thermal Necrosis during Orthopaedic Surgeries. IOP Conf. Series: Mater. Sci. Eng. **1004** (1) (2020)
44. Dahibhate, R.V., Jaju, S.B., Sarode, R.I.: Development of mathematical model for prediction of bone drilling temperature. Materials Today: Proceedings **38**, 2732 (2020)
45. RavekarK., Jaju S.: Design and analysis of material discharge plate of microsurfacing machine, Materials Today: Proceedings, vol. 38 ,pp. 2385 (2020)
46. Jaju, S.B., Charkha, P.G., Kale, M.: Gas metal arc welding process parameter optimization for AA7075 T6. J. Phys. Conf. Ser. **1**, 2021 (1913)
47. DhakneA.,Jaju S., Shukla S., Review on analysis of enhancing wear properties through thermo-mechanical treatment and grain size, Materials Today: Proceedings, 60,pp.2270, 2022
48. Deshmukh, B.B., Jaju, S.B.: Design and analysis of glass fiber reinforced polymer (GFRP) leaf spring. In: International Conference on Emerging Trends in Engineering and Technology, ICETET , pp. 82 (2011)
49. Park, W.R., Jang, J.H.: An inexpensive and rapid method for removal of multiple stripped locking screws following locking plating: a case report. Int. J. Surg. Case Rep. **57**, 1347 (2019)
50. Kumar, A., Saini, M., Jameel, J., Khan, R.: "Turn the tail, not the head": a simple, quick and inexpensive technique for the safe removal of jammed/stripped locking screws. Eur. J. Orthop. Surg. Traumatol. **30**, 1119–1123 (2020)
51. Prabhakar, S.M., Decruz, J., James, W.L.H., Kunnasegaran, R.: A simple technique for removal of interlocking screw from an intramedullary nail: a case report, Vol. 11, Issue 1, pp. 12–15 JOCR January (2021)
52. Maffulli, N., et al.: J. Orthop. Surg. Res. **15**, 478 (2020)
53. Ren, M., Yi, P.H.: Artificial intelligence in orthopedic implant model classification: a systematic review. Skeletal Radiol. **51**(2), 407–416 (2021). https://doi.org/10.1007/s00256-021-038 84-8

Analytic Algorithm for Predicting Diabetes Based on GSDRC-Stacking-Anchor Model

Jiaxin Jiang$^{(\boxtimes)}$ and Yanhui Zhou

Faculty of Computer and Information Science, Southwest University, Chongqing 400715, China
1316090947@qq.com

Abstract. "How to prevent diabetes" has become a global issue that is addressed as the incidence of diabetes keeps rising quickly and the number of deaths from complications keeps rising. The majority of researchers right now concentrate on model performance optimization, ignoring the study of decision transparency and interpretability, which limits the field's ability to be widely applied to highly risk choice scenarios like diabetes prediction. Due to the great internal complexity of the models, the accuracy of highly interpretable models frequently falls short of expectations in terms of accuracy. We propose the GSDRC-Stacking-Anchor predictive parsing model to overcome the aforementioned shortcomings. First, we suggest a data processing strategy based on the DRC Loss function to address the problems of aberrant feature dimension and unbalanced sample distribution in the original data. The GSDRC parameter optimization algorithm, which is based on theDRC Loss function and the grid search method, is proposed in order to address the problems that the traditional grid search algorithm is not applicable to data samples with unbalanced distribution and the tuning parameters time is too long for the model. Last but not least, the GSDRC-Stacking-Anchor interpretable prediction model is proposed, and the Stacking integrated learning method and interpretable Anchor algorithm are introduced on the basis of a single prediction model after parameter optimization. This method can significantly reduce the workload of physicians, help doctors make preventive decisions, and improve patients' self testing and prevention abilities, as well as provide a direction for some future medical research.

Keywords: GSDRC algorithm · Model fusion · Interpretable Anchor algorithm · Analysis of diabetes prediction

1 Introduction

The consumption of high-carbohydrate, high-fat junk food has gradually become a common way of life, and as a result, more and more people have adapted to the "fast food" lifestyle as the global economy and people's standard of living have advanced [1]. As a result, diabetes is developing at an earlier and earlier age, and its symptoms and chronic complications are beginning to show up. Around 5 million individuals worldwide die of diabetes complications each year, accounting for 8.2% of all fatalities, and diabetes complications are the primary factor contributing to the higher mortality in diabetic

© The Author(s), under exclusive license to Springer Nature Switzerland AG 2024
S. Ponnusamy and V. R. Bora (Eds.): AIBTR 2023, CCIS 1987, pp. 39–54, 2024.
https://doi.org/10.1007/978-3-031-49454-3_3

patients [2]. Diabetes is currently recognized as the most helpless "killer" in modern medicine because it is a lifelong, incurable condition.

Foreign academics have already investigated diabetes prognosis. Decision trees were used by Yue Huang and Paul McCullagh [3] in 2004 to achieve prediction accuracy of 78%; in 2008, Huy Nguyen and Evangelos [4] proposed a novel method HBA with support vector machine (SVM), artificial neural network (ANN), or decision tree (DT) together to improve classification accuracy; and in 2020, Md. Kamrul Hasan and Dola Das et al. [5] proposed to perform a weighted combination of various ML models, with integrated classification having the best.In 2022,Chandrashekhar Azad and Bharat Bhushan [6] using the PIDD dataset and proposed classifying diabetes synthetic SMOTE algorithm, genetic algorithm, and decision tree, achieving a considerable accuracy of 82.1256%.

Domestic research on computerized diabetes prediction only recently began. Meiying Zhu and Liling Xu [7] employed decision tree analysis to create a diabetes prediction model in 2008.In 2018,Chunchun Cui [8] researched an improved BP neural network as an algorithm, which handled the problem of highly simple convergence to local minima and chronological issue of irregular data; Chunfu Zhang [9] proposed the GA-XGBoost prediction model in 2020, using genetic algorithms to set the XGBoost model's parameters to obtain the optimal combination of parameters, and using the integration method for decision trees, support vector machines, random forests, and other base classifiers integration to further enhance the prediction effect; In 2022,Wang Min and Xu Yinghao [10] et al. proposed to improve the genetic algorithm for the problem that the genetic algorithm is easy to fall into the local optimal and the IGABP algorithm with ameliorated genetic algorithm selection operator and adaptive genetic algorithm crossover and variance probability formula.Experiments showed that their model works best.

The research on diabetes prediction has been a popular topic in recent years, and diabetes prediction is one of the top objectives, according to the domestic and international literature on the subject. Most researchers in the field of diabetes prediction currently concentrate on improving model performance, ignoring the study of decision transparency and explainability, which limits its widespread applicability in high-risk decision scenarios like diabetes prediction. Because models are so internally complex, high-precision models fre-quently perform poorly in terms of interpretability, and highly interpreta-ble models frequently forecast accuracy perform with insufficient accuracy. According to the aforementioned research, no interpretable algorithms for disease prediction have yet been developed. For output decisions to be translated into language that humans can understand, highly accurate and interpretable models are essential. This is a challenging task for the computer and medical industries, and there is enormous research potential. Our proposed GSDRC-Stacking-Anchor predictive parsing model propose has good predictive parsing performance, which effectively reduces the workload of doctors, helps doctors make preventive decisions, enhances patients' capacity for self-testing and prevention, as well as provide a direction for some future medical research.

2 Related Work

2.1 Datasets

All of the data for the experiment were taken from the physical examination data of the tertiary hospital. The total number of data sample case individuals was 3244, and there were 93 feature fields for each case individual, including 92 feature indicators and 1 feature label. Characteristics included insulin resistance index HIR, retinol-binding protein-4, triglycerides, BMI, ultrasensitive C-reactive protein, leukocytometry, single nucleotide polymorphisms, family history of DM, and glucose levels. Characteristics marked as 0 for healthy and 1 for unhealthy.

Table 1. Overview of some diabetes physical examination data sets.

Id	RBP4	TG	HIR	hsCRP	Wbc	SNP37	Glucose	lable
1	10.92	2.4	1.5748	2.08	0	1	148	0
2	33.84	1.18	1.5644	4.95	8.88	1	85	1
3	53.69	3.93	1.7155	10	8.34	2	183	1
4	20.37	2.52	1.9609	1.16	11.17	3	89	0
5	33.75	2.12	1.0002	13.21	6.8	1	137	1
...	...	...	...	...	...	...	...	...

Positive and negative sample imbalance has an impact on the model performance training, the model is difficult to extract feature patterns in a small number of sample classes, and overfitting occurs because the model is trained on a limited number of sample classes. The original hospital diabetes physical examination dataset suffers from positive and negative sample imbalance,with a ratio of approximately 5:2 (Fig. 1).

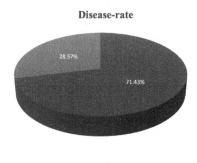

Fig.1. Prevalence distribution of diabetes data set. The graph shows 71.43% of positive samples and 28.57% of negative samples.

2.2 Model Performance Indicators

The confusion matrix, which consists of four potential outcomes for both anticipated and actual samples, was developed in order to assess the algorithmic model's final performance.

Table 2. Confusion Matrix.

Anticipate Actual	Positive	Negative
Positive	TP(True Positive)	FN(False Negative)
Negative	FP(False Positive)	TN(True Negative)

In the confusion matrix, the symbols TP and TN stand for the patient being genuinely ill and the model's forecast of being ill, respectively. This illustrates how closely the model's prediction matches the reality.FN denotes a missed diagnosis in which the patient is ill and the model predicts that the patient is not ill; FP is a misdiagnosis in which the patient is not ill and the model predicts that the patient is ill.

The confusion matrix can be used to obtain six metrics for model performance: Accuracy, Recall, Precision, F1, AUC value, and ROC curve.

$$\text{Precision} = \frac{TP}{TP + FP} \tag{1}$$

$$\text{Recall} = \frac{TP}{TP + FN} \tag{2}$$

$$\text{Accuracy} = \frac{TP + TN}{TP + FP + FN + TN} \tag{3}$$

$$F1 = \frac{2 \cdot \text{Precision} \cdot \text{Recall}}{\text{Precision} + \text{Recall}} \tag{4}$$

where Precision is the precision rate, which is the proportion of actual disease in the group of samples that the model predicts to be ill.Accuracy is represents the proportion of accurate predictions made by the model in all cases; F1 is referred to as the harmonic mean, and takes a value between 0 and 1. Recall is the recall rate, which represents the proportion of real illnesses that are successfully predicted by the model in the sample set of real illnesses. F1 is suggested as a solution to balance the precision rate and recall rate because it is difficult to measure to quantify the impact of the model's performance when there is a conflict between the two.

The subject operating characteristic curve, also known as the ROC curve, is a curve made up of a true-positive rate in the vertical coordinate and a false-positive rate in the horizontal coordinate. AUC is a criterion based on the ROC curve, known as the Area Under Curve (AUC), geometrically the size of the area surrounded by the ROC curve and the straight line x = 1, the coordinate axis, the value of which ranges from 0 to 1, the larger the value indicates that the model predicts better, and vice versa [11].

In conclusion, as F1 and AUC are more thorough measures of the performance effects of predictive models, we uses them as its benchmarks for measuring such effects.

3   Data Processing Based OnDRC Loss Function

The cross-entropy loss function [12], which is frequently employed in binary classification issues, is used to calculate the separation between two sample distributions and offers the benefits of quick convergence and quick learning. The cross-entropy loss function, however, only takes into account differences between classes and ignores differences between samples within classes. If the measure between samples of the same class is greater than the measure of samples of different classes, and the samples of different classes are too similar, this can result in misclassification. In order to effectively raise the inter-class variability, the central loss function (Center Loss) [13] is added, it is employed to decrease intra-class variance. Following is a succinct explanation of the central loss function's basic theory: Samples inside a class are determined to be clustered toward the center by calculating their proximity to the center of the class, rewarding samples close to the center and punishing samples far from the center. Because it is important to account for both differences across classes and differences within classes,the cross-entropy loss function is used in conjunction with the central loss function, whose expression formula is:

$$L = L_C + \beta L_m = -\sum_{i=1}^{n} \log\left(\frac{e^{H_{y_i}^T + a_{y_i}}}{\sum_{j=1}^{m} e^{H_j^T x_j + b_j}}\right) + \frac{\beta}{2}\sum_{i=1}^{n}|x_i - m_{y_i}|_2^2 \quad (5)$$

where $x_i \in R^d$ denotes the i-th depth feature of class y_i, $m_{y_i} \in R^d$, which is denoted as the class center of class y_i feature x_i, and its value varies with x_i.

The loss function is affected by the ratio of positive to negative sample outputs, and the cross-entropy loss function iterates slowly and is susceptible to the problem of local optimum. The basic idea of DR Loss is to transform the classification problem into a confidence ranking problem, which optimizes the confidence distribution of sample pairs (containing one positive and one negative sample) in the dataset to solve the intra-class positive and negative sample imbalance problem. In order to solve the intra-class positive and negative sample imbalance problem,We proposes to use the Distribu-tional Ranking Loss (DR Loss) [14] to replace the cross-entropy loss function and the Center Loss function. Distributional Ranking Loss and Center Loss are combined as theDRC Loss function with the following equation:

$$L = L_{DR} + \beta L_m = \frac{1}{L}\sum_i^{n} \log(1 + \exp(L_Z))\left(\hat{P}_{i,-} - \hat{P}_{i,+} + \gamma\right) + \frac{\beta}{2}\sum_{i=1}^{n}|x_i - m_{y_i}|_2^2 \quad (6)$$

where $\hat{P}_{i,+}$ is the minimization of the positive sample distribution and $\hat{P}_{i,-}$ is the maximization of the negative sample distribution, with a fixed value of 0.5 to ensure accurate differentiation between positive and negative samples.

After feature processing based on the DRC Loss function, the high-dimensional original feature dataset is visualized and exhibited using the UMAP dimensionality reduction technique to produce the positive and negative sample distribution maps shown in Figs. 2 and 3, respectively.

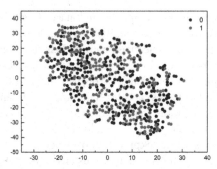

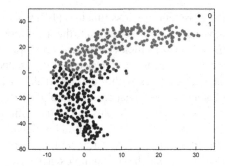

Fig.2. Before Data Processing. It shows the distribution of samples withoutDRC Loss function data processing, with indistinguishable positive and negative sample confusion and within-class sample discretization

Fig.3. After Data Processing. It shows the distribution of samples processed by theDRC Loss function data, with positive and negative samples being distributed in a linear partitioned data differentiation, and the effect of compact and non-loose intra-class sample measure

We can infer from Figs. 2 and 3 above that theDRC Loss function has remarkable effects on how the data is processed.

4   GSDRC-Stacking-Anchor Predictive Analytic Model

In this section, we will use Adaboost [15], Gradient Boosting [16], XGBoost [17], LightGBM [18], and BPNN [19] to compare with our algorithm for experiments on predictive ablations.

Default values were used for the hyperparameters of the basic models, and the ROC curves for the five basic models on the data set are shown in Fig. 4:

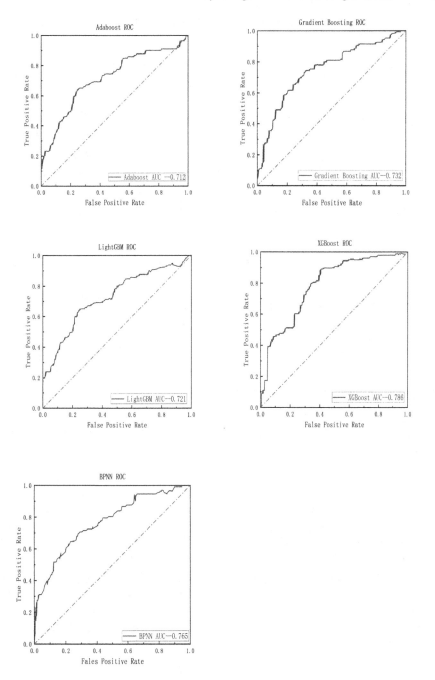

Fig. 4. ROC curves of five basic models. It shows the predictive effect of five basic models, including roc curves and auc values

The F1 and AUC values for the five basic models are shown in the table:

Table 3. Basic Model Experimental Results.

Activation	Prediction model	F1	AUC	Time(s)
Before parameters optimization	Adaboost	0.710	0.712	133
	Gradient Boosting	0.692	0.732	142
	XGBoost	0.794	**0.786**	128
	LightGBM	0.738	0.721	157
	BPNN	**0.801**	0.765	**112**

Table 3 shows that BPNN exhibits the most impressive performance in terms of F1 value, and that XGBoost's impact is much greater than that of the other four models in terms of AUC. No matter which model has an F1 and AUC score below 0.85, the running duration is excessive, the manifestation effectiveness is unsatisfactory, and more model optimization is required to enhance the model's performance effect.

It takes a lot of time and effort to artificially adjust each model parameter to adapt to the taken value and select the optimal parameter combination because the parameters of algorithms like BPNN and XGBoost are numerous and take different values. Therefore, we uses the grid search algorithm (GridSearchCV) [20] for the best parameter selection. Due to the traditional grid search algorithm's cross-validation component's inapplicability to data with an unbalanced proportion of sample categories, the GSDRC parameter optimization method—based on the grid search algorithm and theDRC Loss function—is proposed. The following are the fundamental principles of GSDRC parameter optimization:

(1) To complete the grid search phase, the parameters are randomly organized into "grids" and input one at a time into the model training.
(2) The original data is processed byDRC Loss function to obtain a balanced data set with positive and negative ratios, which is divided according to the ratio of 4:1, of which 4 parts are used as training set for model training and 1 part is used as test set to verify the model effect, and the final model AUC value is obtained.

The optimal parameter combinations of XGBoost, Adaboost, Gradient Boosting, LightGBM, and BPNN are obtained by the GSDRC parameter optimization method. Due to the space limitation, the optimization process is not introduced in detail, and only the optimal parameter combinations after optimization by the GSDRC method are shown. Among them, the optimal parameters of each model are shown in Table 4 below.

Table 4. Optimal parameters of the basic model.

model	Parameter	Optimal parameters
XGBoost	learning_rate	0.1
	n_estimators	100
	gamma	0.2
	max_depth	4
	min_child_weight	2
Adaboost	n_estimators	170
	learning_rate	0.21
	max_depth	8
Gradient Boosting	learning_rate	0.1
	n_estimators	50
LightGBM	max_depth	13
	min_split_gain	0.045
	num_leaves	103
	alpha	0.83
BPNN	lr	0.1
	epochs	100
	show	20
	mc	0.8
	goal	0.001

As a result, the ROC curves for GSDRC-XGBoost, GSDRC-Adaboost, GSDRC-Gradient Boosting, GSDRC-LightGBM, and GSDRC-BPNN can be obtained, and they are displayed in Fig. 5 below:

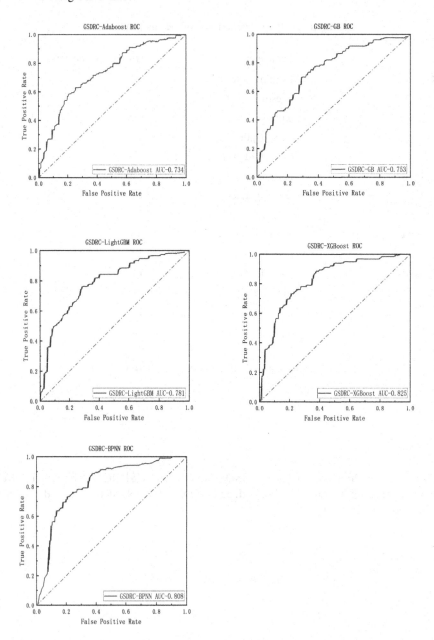

Fig. 5. Five ROC curves after GSDRC parameter optimization processing. It shows the prediction results of five basic models after GSDRC tuning, including roc curves and auc values

The corresponding experimental results are shown in the following table:

Table 5. Model experimental results after optimizing GSDRC parameters.

Activtion	Prediction model	F1	AUC	Time(s)
After parameters optimization	GSDRC-Adaboost	0.774(+6.4%)	0.734(+2.2%)	117(+25)
	GSDRC-Gradient Boosting	0.744(+5.2%)	0.753(+2.1%)	133(+41)
	GSDRC-XGBoost	0.820(+2.6%)	**0.825(+3.9%)**	105(+13)
	GSDRC-LightGBM	0.798(+6.0%)	0.781(+6.0%)	138(+46)
	GSDRC-BPNN	**0.823(+2.2%)**	0.808(+4.3%)	**101 (+9)**

The aforementioned graphs demonstrate that the base model's running time 、ROC curve value, F1, and AUC has enhanced after GSDRC parameter optimization. From the above graphs, it can be seen that the runtime of the base model after GSDRC parameter optimization has upgraded in both ROC curve values and F1 and AUC, thus proving that GSDRC parameter optimization does have the ability to enhanced the model effect. Experimentation bring in the idea of integrated learning stacking on this premise in order to further increase the prediction capacity of the model, because to the restricted effectiveness of F1, AUC, and running time elevation. The final stacking layers are two levels, with GSDRC-XGBoost, GSDRC-Adaboost, GSDRC-Gradient Boosting, and GSDRC-LightGBM chosen as the first layer's base learners and GSDRC-BPNN as the second layer's meta-learners. The steps involved in building a GSDRC-Stacking predictive model are as follows:

(1) The initial data set is put through DRC Loss function feature optimization before being separated into a training set and a test set in a 7:3 ratio.
(2) To build the GSDRC-Stacking prediction model, GSDRC-XGBoost, GSDRC-Adaboost, GSDRC-Gradient Boosting, and GSDRC-LightGBM are chosen as the first layer's base learners, while GSDRC-BPNN is utilized as the second layer's meta-learners.
(3) The training set data outputted by the base learner will be used as part of the sample data of the input meta-learner data, and a new matrix is formed as the training set of the meta-learner after 5 times cross-validation, while the test set of the meta-learner is combined by summing the mean values according to the 5 times output matrix.
(4) The model's final output prediction results are derived from the meta-learner's output results.

The GSDRC-Stacking's prediction results are compared with the models of XGBoost, Adaboost, Gradient Boosting, LightGBM, and BPNN optimized by GSDRC parameters, with the comparison results presented in Table 4. The prediction results are displayed below in Fig. 6 as the ROC curve for the GSDRC-Stacking prediction model.

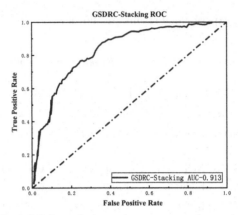

Fig. 6. GSDRC-Stacking ROC Curve. It shows the roc curve and auc value of 0.913 for GSDRC-Stacking

Table 6. Comparison of GSDRC-Stacking Prediction Model Experiments.

Prediction model	F1	AUC	Time(s)
GSDRC-Adaboost	0.774(-10.1%)	0.734(-17.9%)	117(+25)
GSDRC-Gradient Boosting	0.744(-13.1%)	0.753(-16.0%)	133(+41)
GSDRC-XGBoost	0.820(-5.5%)	0.825(-8.8%)	105(+13)
GSDRC-LightGBM	0.798(-7.7%)	0.781(-13.2%)	138(+46)
GSDRC-BPNN	0.823(-5.2%)	0.808(-10.5%)	101(+9)
GSDRC-Stacking	**0.875***	**0.913***	**92***

Taking into account the top three model metrics of F1, AUC, and running time, it can be inferred from Table 6 that the prediction performance of the GSDRC-Stacking model is greatly enhanced after utilizing the Stacking integration idea. Therefore, the GSDRC-Stacking model, the prediction model is constructed. GSDRC-Stacking conduct comparison experiments with the PMSGD model proposed by Chandrashekhar Azad [6] and the DBNLDA model proposed by Manu Madhavan [21] in the previous two years in order to fully validate the effect of the model. As can be seen from Table 7, the GSDRC-Stacking diabetes dataset performs the best in these comparison experiments.

Table 7. Comparative Experiment of Related Prediction Models.

Prediction model	F1	AUC	Time(s)
PMSGD	0.811(-6.4%)	0.795(-11.8%)	125(+33)
DBNLDA	0.736(-13.9%)	0.842(-7.1%)	160(+67)
GSDRC-Stacking	**0.875***	**0.913***	**92***

In order to guarantee the prediction performance effect without destroying the internal structure of the prediction model, but also to explain the behavior of the high performance prediction model, experiment introduces the post hoc explainable model Anchor [22] to construct the prediction resolution GSDRC-Stacking-Anchor model. The Anchor algorithm will look at the change in the prediction effect after perturbing the attributes of a subset of the features to find the anchor point. According to the theory, it finds a minimum feature subset inside the set of features that yields the same prediction outcomes for all sample instances, at which time the minimum feature subset serves as the black box model anchor point that we are seeking for.

$$\mathbb{E}_{D(z|A)}\left[1_{f(x)=f(z)}\right] \geq \tau, A(x) = 1 \tag{7}$$

In the anchor point Eq. 7, x represents the sample individuals in the diabetes data set; f represents the GSDRC-Stacking prediction black box model to be explained. When the input diabetes sample entity corresponds to the sample in the feature subset, then A(x) = 1 is established at this point, and A represents the minimum feature rule set we are looking for, which is the anchor point.

Equation 8 illustrates a trade-off procedure for the accuracy and coverage of its model decision, which aims to maximize Coverage while maintaining Precision at a predetermined threshold and enhancing the generalizability of the model explanation.

$$\underset{(A \text{ s.t. } (prec(A) \geq \tau) \geq}{\max} \; \underset{1 - \delta}{COV(A)} \tag{8}$$

The GSDRC-Stacking-Anchor interpretable prediction model process is shown as follows:

(1) Build GSDRC-Stacking process steps (1)-(4)
(2) The predicted results using GSDRC-Stacking are combined with the sample individual instances to form a new data set.
(3) Anchor extracts the nodes activated and the rules satisfied during the GSDRC-Stacking classification prediction, and the actual classification path of this failed sample consists of a series of extracted rules, and returns this rule set and the precision and coverage. (The p% precision represents the p% probability that other samples in the same rule set as the failed sample are classified as failed samples by the GSDRC-Stacking black box prediction model, and the c% coverage represents the overall sample of c% samples satisfying the rule)
(4) The returned rule set of the ensemble minimum feature is the GSDRC-Stacking anchor point of the black box model, and the GSDRC-Stacking-Anchor model is constructed.

5   Experimental Results

Since the interpretable Anchor algorithm is a post hoc local interpretation algorithm, in this section we will analyze some of the outputs of the GSDRC-Stacking-Anchor model, as shown in Fig. 7 below.

```
If {Glucose<7 And HIR <2.69} then Predict{0} Precision 96% Coverage 18%
If {Glucose>13 And HIR=<2.69 And SNP37=2 And DM=3 And hsCRP>10} then Predict{1} Precision 98% Coverage 23%
If {Glucose>=13 And And DM>=2 And hsCRP>10} then Predict{1} Precision 96% Coverage 23%
If {30<AST<40 And CHO<=5.17  And 0.9<TG<1.8 } then Predict{1} Precision 89% Coverage 23%
If {Glucose<4 And SNP37=2 And DM=2 } then Predict{1} Precision 93% Coverage 19%
If {4<Glucose<10 And SNP37=1} then Predict{0} Precision 91% Coverage 22%
If {SNP37=3 And 40<RBP4<50 And 年龄=6 And 7<Glucose<10} then Predict{1} Precision 90% Coverage 27%
If {HIR<2.69 And 120<Cr<150 And 7<wbc<10 } then Predict{1} Precision 97% Coverage 21%
If {Glucose>13 And HIR <2.69} then Predict{0} Precision 96% Coverage 25%
If {10<Lpa<140 And hsCRP<10 And Glucose>13} then Predict{1} Precision 97% Coverage 20%
```

Fig. 7. Partial output results of GSDRC-Stacking-Anchor model. It includes GSDRC-Stacking-Anchor model prediction resolution results, coverage, accuracy

According to Fig. 7, Anchor's interpretation of the GSDRC-Stacking model for predicting disease was that glutathione transaminase was in the range of 30–40, triglycerides were in the range of 0.9–1.8 and cholesterol was less than or equal to 5.17, all of which were in the normal range, with a coverage of 23% and an accuracy of 89%. A 6-year-old child was predicted to be ill with a retinol binding protein of 40–50, single nucleotide polymorphism and blood glucose in the normal range, with a coverage rate of 27% and an accuracy rate of 90%; a user who was predicted to be ill gave an explanation: serum creatinine of 120–150, insulin resistance factor and white blood cell values in the normal range, with a coverage rate of 21% and an accuracy rate of 97%. The GSDRC-Stacking-Anchor model prediction analysis that the majority of the cases of sicken are that the physical characteristic values are within the normal range, which requires us to pay attention to the effect of the combination of case characteristics on the prevalence of diabetes. However, it should be noted that the model's explanations are not always accurate, so the prediction analysis produced by the GSDRC-Stacking-Anchor model does not replace the doctor's decision-making; rather, it can only support it by helping the doctor make judgments about the patient's condition and provide appropriate preventive advice, as well as by increasing the doctor's productivity, lowering the rate of misdiagnosis, reduce the prevalence of diabetes effectively. Finally, the results of running the current diabetes dataset based on the GSDRC-Stacking- Anchor model suggest that the medical field could focus in the future on the effects of glutathione-triglyceride-cholesterol, retinol-binding protein-mononucleotide polymorphism-glycemia, serum creatinine and leukocytes on the prevalence of diabetes and that more data need to be collected to further validate whether they continue to follow the same distribution.

6   Conclusion

The GSDRC-Stacking-Anchor model provides decision explanation of the model operation while ensuring the classification accuracy of the model, so that the black-box prediction model can combine high accuracy and interpretability at the same time. GSDRC-Stacking-Anchor interpretable prediction model effectively reduces physicians' workload, assists physicians in preventive decision-making, improves patients' self-testing ability and prevention ability, and also provides a certain degree of help for future research directions in the medical field.

In this thesis, improvements have been made in terms of model effects, but there are still some shortcomings, and the following are the directions for optimization and enhancement of the study:

(1) The results of the GSDRC-Stacking-Anchor model proposed running the current diabetes dataset revealed that glutathione-triglyceride-cholesterol, retinol-binding protein-mononucleotide polymorphism-glycemia, serum creatinine, and leukocytes have some influence on the prevalence of diabetes. However, more data must be collected in the future to further confirm whether they continue to follow the same distribution.
(2) Images are also a popular research direction in the medical field, and the GSDRC-Stacking-Anchor model can be used in the future for predictive resolution of pathological images to make more contributions to disease prevention.

References

1. Men, Y.,Zheng S.: Study on the changes of 12 hour ambulatory blood glucose in patients with type 2 diabetes mellitus with different fasting C-peptide levels based on the midnight noon ebb flow theory. Clinical Research of Traditional Chinese Medicine,1–7 (2023)
2. Guo, H.,Ren, J.,Hou, X.: Prediction of type 2 diabetic nephropathy based on Optimized Neural Network.Health Vocational Education (2023)
3. Huang, Y., McCullagh, P.: Evaluation of outcome prediction for a clinical diabetes database. KELSI **2004**, 181–190 (2022)
4. NAPham, H., Triantaphyllou, E.: Prediction of diabetes by employing a new data mining approach which balances fitting and generalization. Comput. Inform. Sci. **2008,** 11–26 (2018)
5. Kamrul, H., Ashraful, A., Dola, D., Eklas, H., Mahmudul, H.: Diabetes prediction using ensembling of different machine learning classifiers. IEEE Access **8**, 76516–76531 (2020)
6. Chandrashekhar, A.,Bharat, B., Sharma, R.:Prediction model using SMOTE: genetic algorithm and decision tree (PMSGD) for classification of diabetes mellitus. Multim. Syst. **4**, 1289–1307 (2022)
7. Zhu, M., Xu, L., Zhu, Y.: Establishment of decision tree model for screening high-risk population of diabetes mellitus using health records data. Chinese Primary Health Care **5**, 50–53 (2008)
8. Cui, C.: Research on prediction system of diabetic complications based on Neural Network. Beijing Jiaotong University (2018)
9. Zhang, C.: Application of machine learning algorithm based on parameter optimization in diabetes prediction. SouthWest University of Science and Technology (2020)
10. Wang, M., Xu, Y., Zhu, X.: Prediction model of diabetes complications based on improved genetic algorithm and optimized BP neural network .Comput. Modern. **327**, 69–74 (2022)
11. Khemakhem, S., Boujelbene, Y.: Predicting credit risk on the basis of financial and non-financial variables and data mining. Rev. Acc. Financ. **17**(3), 316–340 (2018)
12. Li, L.,Milos, D.,Murray, H.: Approximating the gradient of cross-entropy loss function. IEEE Access, pp.99 (2020)
13. Wen, Y., Zhang, K., Li, Z., et al.: A discriminative feature learning approach for deep face recognition. In: European Conference on Computer Vision. In: Proceedings of SIGI. Berkley, pp. 227–234 (2016)
14. Qian, Q., Chen, L., Li, H., et al.: DR loss: improving object detection by distributional ranking. Comput. Sci. **5**, 99–110 (2019)

15. Ma, J.: Design and implementation of a diabetes prediction system based on Django framework.Yunnan Normal University,YunNan (2021)
16. Li, Y.: A deep learning-based prediction model for gestational diabetes. Qingdao University of Science and Technology, China (2021)
17. Chen, T., He, T., Benesty, M., et al.: Xgboost: extreme gradient boosting. R Package Version **4**, 1–4 (2015)
18. Wang,Y.: Research and Application of Classification Prediction Algorithm Based on Improved LightGBM, Beijing Institute of Petrochemical Technology,China (2022)
19. Zhou, M., et al.: Application of artificial neural networks to predict birth weight of newborns with gestational diabetes, Association for Computing Machinery, New York, pp. 175–186 (2018)
20. Zhu, N., Zhu, C., Zhou, L., Zhu, Y., Zhang, X.: Optimization of the random forest hyper-parameters for power industrial control systems intrusion detection using an improved grid search algorithm. Appl. Sci. **12**(20), 173–185 (2022)
21. Manu,M., Gopakumar,G.: DBNLDA: Deep Belief Network based representation learning for lncRNA-disease association prediction. Appl. Intell. **5**, 5342–5352 (2022)
22. Ribeiro, Marco,T., Sameer, S.,Carlos, G. Anchors: high-precision model-agnostic explanations. In: Proceedings of the AAAI Conference on Artificial Intelligence. **32**(1), 426–434 (2018)

Detection and Analysis of Gait Impairments in Lower Back Pain (LBP) Patients Using Image Processing Techniques

P. Praveen[1]($\boxtimes$) (ID), M. S. Mallikarjunaswamy[1] (ID), and S. Chandrashekara[2]

[1] Department of Electronics and Instrumentation, Sri Jayachamarajendra College of Engineering, JSS Science and Technology University, Mysuru, India
ppraveen26@gmail.com
[2] ChanRe Rheumatology and Immunology Center and Research, Bengaluru, India

Abstract. Every person has a unique gait, which is the pattern of individuals walking. Doctors can explore health conditions of an individual by studying stride, as many health issues reveal distinct gait manifestations. The posture of a person's spine, neck, shoulder, and upper limbs has a big impact on gait. Lower back discomfort is a condition that significantly affects gait irregularity. Patients with persistent lower back pain (LBP) typically struggle to walk and move more slower than people who are healthy. Patients with LBP typically walk with more coordinated pelvic and thoracic spins than healthy individuals. In these cases, low thorax-pelvis relative phase seems to have an impact on arm swing. It is crucial to study the characteristics of gait in order to comprehend gait disorders. The currently used techniques use infrared cameras for motion detection, retroreflective tags, and micro electro mechanical sensors. The relevant literature is presented in this work, and the methodology adopted to achieve the goal of creating an image-processing technique-based non-invasive method to extract gait features is narrated. The procedure entails recording of the video with a mobile device and processing it for the extraction of the gait features. After the background is removed from the video frames, silhouettes are extracted. Tags are marked on the silhouette to understand and the characteristics of the human gait are measured. The dataset is created under medical supervision for normal and five forms of abnormal gaits namely spastic gait, scissors gait, steppage gait, waddling gait, and propulsive gait—six features relating to distance and angular measurements are retrieved. In this investigation, LBP was found to cause an aberrant waddling gait. The steps involved in the procedure are non-invasive, and the process of video recording needs no additional effort from the impaired person under test. The observed features in this study are found helpful for analysis of LBP. The developed procedure can be extended for analysis of arthritis and other disorders that cause gait impairment.

Keywords: Gait features · Silhouette extraction · Image Processing · Arthritis · Low back pain

S. Ponnusamy and V. R. Bora (Eds.): AIBTR 2023, CCIS 1987, pp. 55–70, 2024.
https://doi.org/10.1007/978-3-031-49454-3_4

1 Introduction

Gait can be defined as a manner in which a person walks, it can also be used as one of the parameters to identify an individual as each and every person has a unique gait pattern [1]. Human gait varies due to enormous reasons out of which pain in the lumbar spine usually termed as lower back pain is a major cause. Observation of gait helps the medical professionals in providing early diagnostic hints for disorders like cerebral palsy, Rett syndrome, Parkinson's disease and many more [2]. Gait cycle is described as a series of moments that occur during locomotion and one single gait cycle is called a stride [3]. The Gait cycle has two phases, the first one is swing phase and the second one is stance phase. Swing phase is a phase during which the foot is not in contact with the ground, swing phase begins when the foot leaves the ground and ends when the heel of the same foot strikes the ground [4, 5]. Stance phase consists of all the activities that occur when the foot is in contact with the ground, stance phase begins when heel first touches or strikes the floor and ends when the toe of the same foot is off the floor. Stance phase and swing phase accounts for about 60% and 40% respectively of the gait cycle [6]. All the joints of the lower limbs are involved in gait along with this the posture of the spine, neck, shoulder and upper limbs are also involved in gait [7]. When these body parts that control the manner in which a person walks do not function in a usual way it leads to gait abnormality and these abnormalities can be permanent but by means of physical therapy these abnormalities can be treated or sometimes it gets cured without any medical intervention [8].

There are five basic types of gait abnormalities [9]. These are the common issues found in the subjects

- Spastic gait: This type of gait is characterized by a stiff appearance where the person may drag their feet on the floor while walking.
- Scissors gait: In this type of gait, the legs are bent inwards causing them to crisscross and hit each other while walking.
- Steppage gait: This type of gait is characterized by toes pointing down, which may cause them to scrape the floor while walking.
- Waddling gait: With this type of gait, the person moves side by side and takes very short steps while swinging their body.
- Propulsive gait: This gait is characterized by the neck and head being pushed forward, causing a slouching appearance.

2 Literature Survey

In the literature there are many works relevant to gait analysis and human gait feature extraction are reported. Bogdan et al. [10] have developed an automated system to recognize gait related health problems such as Parkinson's disease, Hemiplegia (paralysis of arm, leg and torso on same side of the body), pain in the leg and pain in the back in elderly individuals, motion is captured using body worn tags and wall mounted sensors and have extracted 13 features to identify those gait related health problems. Michal et al. [11] have adopted a statistical approach for extracting human gait features and used linear discriminant analysis with maximum margin criterion. Matteo et al. [12] developed a system that can recognize a person based on gait. Accelerometer and gyroscope were used to capture the motion signals. Imanne et al. [13] demonstrated an intelligent gait analysis algorithm to detect Parkinson disease and used deep learning methods for gait analysis. In this work they used 18 signals acquired using foot sensors. Daniel et al. [14] have developed an algorithm to detect patellofemoral pain syndrome using a support vector machine classifier. Two sets of features were extracted, one set consisting of 14 ground reaction forces and another set with 16 foot kinematic features.

Ali et al. [15] have proposed a method to calculate the angles made by the joints of upper and lower body parts while walking. The angles of the joint were calculated using Fourier, Gabor, Radon features. Based on these calculations an histogram was developed for each feature individually. Valentina Agostiniet et al. [16] used surface-EMG to record the muscle activity during the gait to interpret the muscle activation patterns in locomotion. Jorge Lattoreet et al. [17] in their study used Microsoft Kinect v2 for motion sensing of the people with irregular gait. The correlation of variable strength between all clinical tests and gait measures are analyzed. Chengtao et al. [18] have proposed an effective method known as consecutive horizontal dropout method for human gait feature extraction. Philippe Terrier [19] experimented with the position of center pressure, recorded on the force platform of the treadmill. In the work of Liang et al. [20] the relevant features were extracted using Fourier transform and Radon transform after which these features were used to train K nearest neighbor classifier. Naveen Rohila [21] have proposed adoptive silhouette extraction method to separate objects like bag, paper, purse etc. from the person's silhouette which will be subjected to gait analysis in order to detect theft or crime. Motion was captured in the form of video on camera. The patients with Lower Back Pain (LBP) often report difficulty in walking. The studies have shown that LBP and gait are meticulously correlated. Yun Peng Huang et al. [22] made a study in which the subjects with lower back pain caused due to herniated discs in the lumbar region (L3-L4-L5-S1) and normal subjects were subjected to gait kinematics study using treadmill test with various speeds and stride lengths. They have shown that the phase relationship between thorax rotations and arm swing was altered in the LBP subjects. Obesity is the major contributor for the chronic LBP. In turn they both seem to affect the gait of a person. Veronica Cimolin [23] and his team has made a quantitative study of the gait pattern of the obese subjects with and without LBP. Obese female subjects with LBP showed longer stance duration and shorter step length compared to the obese and healthy female subjects. The team could demonstrate the association of obesity and LBP affects the gait pattern more than obesity alone. The obese subjects with LBP were characterized by an altered knee and ankle strategy during gait. After studying the literature, the objectives were set to.

1. Develop a non-invasive method to extract features of gait impaired people using image processing techniques.
2. Compare the extracted features of abnormal gait namely spastic gait, scissors gait, steppage gait, waddling gait and propulsive gait with normal gait for analysis.

The developed method is based on capturing video of abnormal human gait, aims to extract human silhouette from images and measures features by marking the tags on the human silhouette extracted. The features extracted are useful in understanding gait impairments in LBP, arthritis and other gait impaired diseases.

3 Proposed System

The most important step in gait analysis is motion capture, for this work the video of normal and abnormal human gaits were recorded in-house at a research lab under medical supervision. Three volunteers were asked to walk back and forth by imitating the 5 different abnormal gaits. The videos were recorded for normal gait, spastic, scissors, waddling, steppage and propulsive abnormal gait pattern under customized laboratory condition. The videos were captured using mobile phone camera at stationary position and with constant background. After recording the video, frames in the video were extracted. The background and foreground image was converted from RGB to HSV scale. Hue Saturation Value (HSV) helps to separate out intensity of the image from colour information of the image, by doing this conversion the special characteristics of the person in image such as head, shape of leg, and hand will be clearly visible. After converting to HSV next step is to subtract the background image with the current frame of the subject, for this image subtraction technique is adopted so that the foreground objects are segmented out from the background. The HSV converted foreground frame and background frame images are bitwise XOR operated as a part of image subtraction. The XOR operated image is converted to gray scale. Binary image is obtained by considering Gray image with threshold greater than 0 as '1' and Gray image with threshold less than or equal to 0 as '0'. The median filter with mask size of [5 × 5] is used to filter the image. The resultant image obtained after background subtraction has all the foreground objects which includes a person's silhouette. The region of interest (ROI) is a person's silhouette whose area is largest compared to other foreground objects, ROI is cropped to extract the silhouette from the obtained image. The silhouette region is obtained through a process known as image segmentation. Image segmentation techniques aim to partition an image into meaningful regions or objects based on their characteristics such as color, intensity, texture, or shape. To obtain the silhouette region, the primary step is often to distinguish the foreground, which represents the object of interest, from the background. This can be achieved by applying thresholding techniques, where a specific threshold value is set to separate the object from the background by differentiating their intensity or color values.

After the initial foreground-background separation, post-processing techniques may be applied to refine the obtained regions and extract the silhouette region specifically. These techniques can involve edge detection algorithms, such as the Canny edge detector, which identifies the boundaries of the object by locating significant changes in pixel intensity. Once the object's edges are identified, additional contour or boundary analysis methods, like the active contour model or region-based algorithms, can be utilized to refine the silhouette region further. These algorithms utilize deformable curve or region models to adapt to the object's boundary, achieving a more precise delineation of the silhouette region. Further, the obtained silhouette is merged with the foreground frame to have silhouette in grayscale in order to improve the identification of image for further processing.

Centroid of the image is calculated as the centroid of the silhouette extracted. And the marker has been inserted for the obtained centroid coordinates. The centroid (X_c, Y_c) of the human silhouette is calculated using the Eqs. (1) and (2).

$$X_c = \frac{1}{N} \sum_{i=1}^{N} X_i \tag{1}$$

$$Y_c = \frac{1}{N} \sum_{j=1}^{N} Y_j \tag{2}$$

where (X_c, Y_c) represents the average contour pixel position, (X_i, Y_j,) represents points on the human blob and N is the total number of points on the contour.

After marking the centroid for the silhouette, the next step is to mark the important tags on the following six parts of the foreground merged silhouettes:

1. right hand
2. left hand
3. right leg
4. left leg
5. chin to neck
6. back of head to spine.

Totally eighteen major tags are marked and the previously marked centroid is also considered as a tag. Three tags must be marked on each of those six parts, marking is done as follows: totally 6 points considering three each on the left hand and right hand (upper arm, elbow and wrist), 6 points considering two each on left leg and right leg along with centroid (ankle, knee and centroid), 3 points considering on chin, starting portion of neck and ending portion of neck, 3 points considering on back portion of head, mid portion of back of neck, and one more on the spine region. The reason to consider three tags on each of these parts is to measure parameters like length and angle made by those parts of the body. The image processing steps involved are depicted in Fig. 1.

Calculation of length and angle using Eqs. (3), (4), (5) and (6): The tags and centroid marks are treated as coordinates (x, y). After marking, the next step is to calculate the following six parameters:

1. The distances between the elbow and the upper arm (RH1), the elbow and the wrist (RH2), and the angle formed by the elbow of the right hand.
2. The distance between the left hand's elbow and the upper arm (LH1), the distance between the elbow and the wrist (LH2), and the angle formed by the elbow.
3. The angle formed by the right leg's knee, the distance from the centroid to the knee (RL1), and the distance from the knee to the ankle (RL2).
4. The angle formed by the left leg's knee, the distance from the centroid to the knee (LL1), and the distance from the knee to the ankle (LL2).
5. The distance from the chin to the beginning of the neck (N1), the distance from the beginning of the neck to the finishing of the neck (N2), and the angle between the chin and neck.
6. The distances between the back of the head and the middle of the neck (S1), the distance between the middle of the neck and the spine area (S2), and the angle between the back of the head and the spine region.

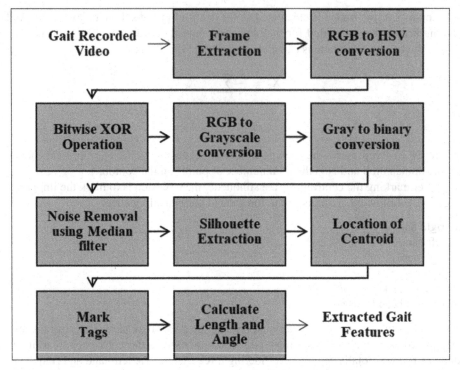

Fig. 1. Image processing steps of gait feature extraction

Since three tags are considered for each parameter, the calculation is carried out in the following way:

Consider three data points $p_1 = (x_1, y_1)$, $p_2 = (x_2, y_2)$, $p_3 = (x_3, y_3)$.

Distance between p_1 and p_2 is used to calculate length d_{12}

$$d_{12} = \sqrt{(x_2 - x_1)^2 + (y_2 - y_1)^2}\,\text{pixels} \tag{3}$$

Distance between p_2 and p_3 gives length d_{23}

$$d_{23} = \sqrt{(x_3 - x_2)^2 + (y_3 - y_2)^2}\,\text{pixels} \tag{4}$$

The angle is calculated as follows:

$$\theta = \left[\left[\tan^{-1}\left(\frac{(y_1 - y_2)}{(x_1 - x_2)}\right) - \tan^{-1}\left(\frac{(y_2 - y_3)}{(x_2 - x_3)}\right)\right] * \frac{180}{\pi}\right] Degrees \tag{5}$$

$$\text{Remaining angle} = (180 - \theta)\text{degrees} \tag{6}$$

Calculations of six parameters result as features of gait for the video processed. These features are useful in understanding the gait impairments.

4   Results and Discussions

The frames are selected from video for feature extraction such that all the parts of the body that affected the normal and abnormal gaits were clearly visible. After this, silhouettes were extracted and centroid was marked on each and every extracted silhouettes. Figure 2 shows images of silhouettes extracted in different gait (a) normal gait (b) propulsive gait (c) waddling gait (d) spastic gait (e) scissors gait (steppage gait). Silhouettes extracted were merged with the foreground frame to have silhouette in greyscale for better visibility and tags marked for calculating features. Figure 3 shows images of tags marked for calculating angles and lengths in different gait (a) normal gait (b) propulsive gait (c) waddling gait (d) spastic gait (e) scissors gait (steppage gait). The lengths measured after marking of tags are recorded and tabulated.

Figure 4 shows the comparison of length measurements between normal and abnormal gaits which is calculated using the Eqs. (3) and (4). Figure 5 shows the comparison of angle measurements between normal and abnormal gaits calculated using Eqs. (5) and (6).

Table 1 depicts length measurements in normal and abnormal cases of gait. Table 2 shows measured angles in degrees for six parameters of normal and abnormal cases of gait and Table 3 angle gives the measurements of head and neck in normal and abnormal cases of gait.

The following observations are made based on this analysis.

1. Normal v/s propulsive: Major dip in the length measurements of LH2, RL1, RL2, LL1, LL2, variation in angle measurement θ at Left hand, right hand & leg and other measurements shows the gait with head and neck pushed along with slouching appearance to the person
2. Normal v/s waddling: Noticeable change in the length measurements RH2 and LL2, angle measurement θ at Right hand and other measurements depict the gait with short steps and with a swinging body. This is a usual characteristic in the subjects with LBP.
3. Normal v/s spastic: The major decrease in the length measurements of LH2, RH2, LL2, variation in the angle measurement θ at left hand & leg and other measurements reveal the dragging of the feet and stiff appearance.
4. Normal v/s scissors: Clear raise in the length measurements of RH2 and LL2, slight variation in the angle measurement θ at right hand, right leg, left hand & left leg and other slight changes in the parameters show the gait with legs bent inwards like crisscross.
5. Normal v/s steppage: Variations in the length parameters like RH2, LH2, RL1, RL2, LL1, N2, S1, variation in the angle measurement θ at the right hand shows the scrapy walk and steppage gait is featured with toes pointing down.

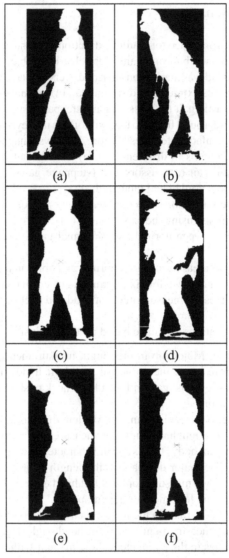

Fig. 2. Silhouettes extracted in different gait (a) Normal gait (b) Propulsive gait (c) Waddling gait (d) Spastic gait (e) Scissors gait (f) Steppage gait

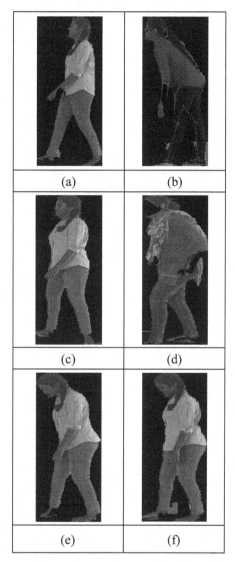

Fig. 3. Tags marked for calculating angles and lengths. (a)Normal gait (b) Propulsive gait (c) Waddling gait (d) Spastic gait (e) Scissors gait (f) Steppage gait

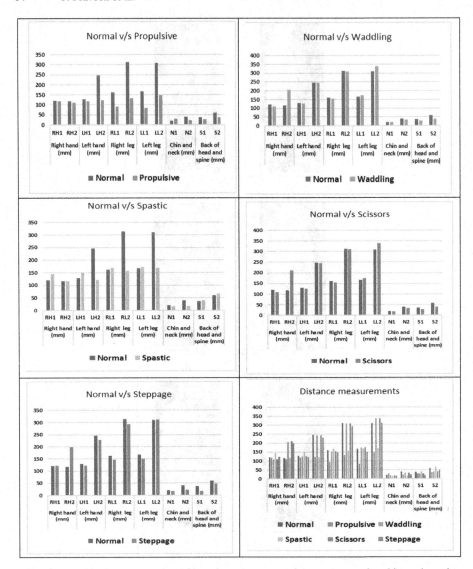

Fig. 4. Graphical representation of length measurements between normal and irregular gaits

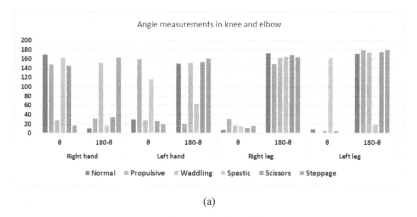

(a)

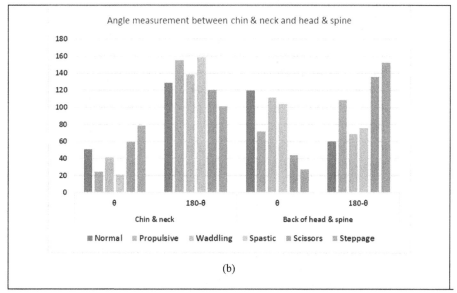

(b)

Fig. 5. (a) Angle variation in knee and elbow (b) Angle measurement between chin & neck and head & spine.

Table 1. Length measurements in normal and abnormal cases of Gait

Sl. No	Gait	Right hand (mm)		Left hand (mm)		Right leg (mm)		Left leg (mm)		Chin and neck (mm)		Back of head and spine (mm)	
		RH1	RH2	LH1	LH2	RL1	RL2	LL1	LL2	N1	N2	S1	S2
1	Normal	120.61	117.00	128.84	246.41	162.15	313.47	167.11	309.30	20.37	40.24	36.99	58.72
2	Propulsive	118.54	109.67	118.84	122.17	91.69	132.50	83.94	147.50	29.08	22.10	27.52	35.98
3	Waddling	109.50	205.73	126.55	244.06	154.99	310.53	174.39	337.55	18.77	33.96	27.62	40.75
4	Spastic	144.86	116.72	149.23	121.53	168.54	157.50	171.72	169.50	15.66	17.10	40.02	65.74
5	Scissors	109.50	210.73	126.55	244.06	154.99	310.53	174.39	337.55	18.77	33.96	27.62	40.75
6	Steppage	122.61	198.97	121.53	228.88	146.10	293.29	150.33	311.57	17.10	23.71	18.24	46.95

Table 2. Angle measurements in normal and abnormal cases of Gait

Gait		Normal	Propulsive	Waddling	Spastic	Scissors	Steppage
Right Hand	θ	169.24	148.55	28.3	162.97	145.13	16.78
	$180-\theta$	10.76	31.44	151.69	17.03	34.86	163.21
Left Hand	θ	29.81	159.79	28.14	116.67	26.162	19.23
	$180-\theta$	150.18	20.2	151.84	63.32	153.83	160.76
Right Leg	θ	7.95	31.1	17.12	14.87	11.2	16.31
	$180-\theta$	172.04	148.89	162.87	165.12	168.79	163.68
Left Leg	θ	8.2	1.2	5.4	161.69	4.61	0.26
	$180-\theta$	171.72	178.79	174.51	18.3	175.38	179.73

Table 3. Angle measurements (head and neck) in normal and abnormal cases of Gait

Gait		Normal	Propulsive	Waddling	Spastic	Scissors	Steppage
Chin and neck	θ	51.09	24.74	41.4	21.17	59.6	78.69
	$180-\theta$	128.9	155.25	138.59	158.82	120.39	101.31
Back of head and Spine	θ	119.53	71.64	111.61	104.16	44.29	27.4
	$180-\theta$	60.47	108.36	68.83	75.84	135.7	152.6

5   Advantages of the Proposed System

The proposed system offers a range of benefits that can revolutionize and streamline healthcare practices. It also holds significant advantages for the medical field in numerous ways. They are:

1. **Non-invasive:** The proposed system does not require any invasive procedures, making it a safe and comfortable method for individuals with gait impairments or other related disorders.
2. **Easy data collection:** The process of recording the video with a mobile device is simple and does not require extensive equipment or technical knowledge. This makes it accessible to a wide range of users.
3. **Minimal assistance required:** The video recording process does not require much assistance from the individual with the impairment. This reduces dependence on others and promotes independence.
4. **Objective measurement:** By extracting silhouettes and measuring specific characteristics of the human walk, the system provides objective measurements of gait. This eliminates subjective biases and allows for more accurate analysis.
5. **Identification of various abnormal gaits:** The system is capable of identifying not only normal gaits but also five different forms of abnormal gaits, including spastic, scissors, steppage, waddling, and propulsive gaits. This broadens the scope of analysis for different disorders.
6. **Comprehensive feature retrieval:** The system retrieves six features related to distance and angular measurements. These features offer valuable insights into gait patterns, aiding in the analysis of gait impairment caused by conditions such as lower back pain (LBP), arthritis, and other disorders.
7. **Potential for diagnosis and treatment monitoring:** The collected features can be instrumental in diagnosing gait impairments and monitoring the progress of treatments or interventions. This can help healthcare professionals make informed decisions regarding patient care.
8. **Scalable and cost-effective:** As the system utilizes readily available mobile devices for video recording, it can be easily scaled up for broader implementation without significant additional costs.
9. **Versatility:** The proposed system can be applied to various conditions causing gait impairments, making it a versatile tool for gait analysis and assessment in different clinical settings.
10. **Potential for early intervention:** By detecting abnormal gaits and measuring gait characteristics, the system has the potential to facilitate early intervention and management of gait impairments. This can lead to better outcomes and improved quality of life for individuals with such conditions.

6 Social Welfare of the Proposed System

The social welfare of the system described focuses on use of gait analysis to understand and potentially diagnose health issues. By studying a person's walking pattern, doctors can gather valuable information about their health, including the presence of conditions like lower back discomfort. This non-invasive method, which involves recording videos and processing them using image-processing techniques, allows for the extraction of gait features that are helpful in analyzing gait disorders. The accessibility and ease of this approach make it beneficial for individuals with impairments, such as lower back pain, arthritis, and other conditions that affect gait. This could be helpful for the rural patients to take the video and send it to other hospitals for analysis. Ultimately, the social welfare aspect lies in providing a cost-effective and efficient means of assessing and managing these health issues, thereby improving the overall well-being of individuals in society.

7 Future Enhancements

In the future, enhancements to the system could include the development of more advanced image-processing techniques to extract additional gait features. This could involve refining the method to accurately measure and analyze aspects of gait such as stride length, foot positioning, and timing of movements. Additionally, incorporating machine learning algorithms could help improve the system's ability to detect and classify different gait abnormalities, allowing for more accurate diagnosis and monitoring of various health conditions. Furthermore, advancements could be made in the hardware used, such as the development of more lightweight and portable devices for video recording, as well as the integration of wearable sensors to provide even more comprehensive data on an individual's gait.

8 Conclusion

The advanced technique utilizes image processing methods to extract gait features in a non-intrusive manner. It employs background subtraction to isolate the human silhouette from the gait sequence, eliminating the need for uncomfortable markers or sensors attached to the individual. These extracted features can be effectively utilized to diagnose gait abnormalities and monitor treatment progress in individuals with impaired walking. The user has the flexibility to attach tags to different body parts, such as the right hand, left hand, right leg, left leg, chin-neck, and back of the head and spine, depending on the situation. Angles and lengths are then calculated for both normal and pathological gaits, reflecting the specific characteristics observed. The study compares key aspects of normal and pathological gaits, including spastic gait, scissors gait, steppage gait, waddling gait, and propulsive gait, for analysis purposes. This investigation successfully identified an aberrant waddling gait as the gait pattern associated with low back pain. The results demonstrate the usefulness of these characteristics in distinguishing between normal and abnormal gaits. Importantly, the method requires minimal intervention when recording videos of individuals with impairments and is easily applicable in laboratory and outpatient settings. These traits can aid in assessing and understanding gait abnormalities in various conditions related to knee, ankle, and hip joints, as well as conditions like lower back pain, arthritis, stroke, and degenerative neurological diseases. Overall, the developed procedure is straightforward, non-invasive, and suitable for use in treating individuals with such conditions.

References

1. Kuo, A.D., Donelan, J.M.: Dynamic principles of gait and their clinical implications. Phys. Ther. **90**(2), 157–174 (2010)
2. Wang, R.: Biomechanical consequences of gait impairment at the ankle and foot: Injury, malalignment, and co-contraction, Technical report, (KTH) Royal Institute of Technology (2012)
3. Chien, H.L., Lu, T.W., Liu, M.W.: Effects of long-term wearing of high-heeled shoes on the control of the body's center of mass motion in relation to the center of pressure during walking. Gait Posture **39**(4), 1045–1050 (2014)
4. Franklin, S., Grey, M.J., Heneghan, N., Bowen, L., Li, F.X.: Barefoot vs common footwear: a systematic review of the kinematic, kinetic and muscle activity differences during walking. Gait Posture **42**(3), 230–239 (2015)
5. Cham, R., Redfern, M.S.: Changes in gait when anticipating slippery floors. Gait Posture **15**(2), 159–171 (2002)
6. Menant, J.C., Steele, J.R., Menz, H.B., Munro, B.J., Lord, S.R.: Effects of walking surfaces and footwear on temporo-spatial gait parameters in young and older people. Gait Posture **29**(3), 392–397 (2009)
7. Kleiner, F.R., Galli, M., Carmo, A.A., Barros, R.M.: Effects of flooring on required coefficient of friction: elderly adult vs. middle-aged adult barefoot gait. Appl. Ergon. **50**, 147–152 (2015)
8. Feltcher, J.: Abnormal Gait: Types, Causes, and Diagnosis. Medical News Today (2017)
9. Pogorelc, B., Bosnić, Z., Gams, M.: Automatic recognition of gait-related health problems in the elderly using machine learning. Multimedia Tools Appl. **58**(2), 333–354 (2012)
10. Pogorelc, B., Bosnic, Z., Gams, M.: Automatic recognition of gait-related health problems in elderly using machine learning. Multimedia Tools Appl. **58**, 333–354 (2012)
11. Balazia, M., Sojka, P.: Gait recognition from motion capture data. ACM Trans. Multimedia Comput. Commun. Appl. **14**(1s), 1–18 (2017)
12. Gadaleta, M., Rossi, M.: IDNet: smartphone-based gait recognition with convolutional neural networks. Pattern Recogn. **74**, 25–37 (2018)
13. El Maachia, I., Bilodeaua, G.-A., Bouachirb, W.: Deep 1D - convnet for accurate Parkinson disease detection and severity prediction from Gait. Exp. Syst. Appl. **143**, 1–27 (2020). Article 113075
14. Lai, D.T.H., Levinger, P., Begg, R.K.: Automatic recognition of gait patterns exhibiting patellofemoral pain syndrome using a support vector machine approach. IEEE Trans. Inf. Technol. Biomed. **13**(5), 810–817 (2009)
15. Saadoon, A., Nordin, M.J.: An automatic human gait recognition system based on joint angle estimation on silhouette images. J. Theoret. Appl. Inf. Technol. **81**(2), 277–284 (2015)
16. Agostini, V., Ghislieri, M., Rosati, S., Balestra, G., Knaflitz, M.: Surface electromyography applied to gait analysis: how to improve its impact in clinics? Front. Neurol. **11**, 1–13 (2020). Article 994
17. Latorre, J., Colomer, C., Alcañiz, M., Llorens, R.: Gait analysis with the Kinect v2: normative study with healthy individuals and comprehensive study of its sensitivity, validity, and reliability in individuals with stroke. J. Neuroeng. Rehabil. **16**(97), 1–11 (2019)
18. Cai, C., Wang, Y.: CHD: consecutive horizontal dropout for human gait feature extraction. In: Proceedings of the International Conference Computing and Pattern Recognition, ICCPR 2019, pp. 89–94 (2019)
19. Terrier, P.: Gait recognition via deep learning of center-of-pressure trajectory. Appl. Sci. **10**, 774 (2020)
20. Wang, L., Tan, T.: Silhouette analysis-based gait recognition for human identification. IEEE Trans. Pattern Anal. Mach. Intell. **25**(12), 1505–1518 (2003)

21. Rohila, N.: Adaptive silhouette extraction and gait recognition in dynamic environments using fuzzy inference system. Int. J. Eng. Res. Technol. **1**(8), 236–243 (2012)
22. Huang, Y.P., Bruijn, S.M., Lin, J.H., Onno, G.: Gait adaptations in low back pain patients with lumbar disc herniation: trunk coordination and arm swing. Eur. Spine J. **20**, 491–499 (2011)
23. Cimolin, V., Vismara, L., Galli, M., Zaina, F., Negrini, S., Capodaglio, P.: Effects of obesity and chronic low back pain on gait. J. Neuroeng. Rehabil. **8**, 1–7 (2011)

MediSecure: A Blockchain-Enabled Ensemble Learning Approach for User-Controlled Single Sign-On and Privacy Preservation in Medical Cyber-Physical Systems

Jagdish F. Pimple[1,2]([✉]) [iD], Avinash Sharma[1,3] [iD], and Jitendra Kumar Mishra[4] [iD]

[1] Department of Computer Science and Engineering, Madhyanchal Professional University, Bhopal, MP, India
`pimplejagdish@gmail.com, jpimple@stvincentngp.edu.in`
[2] Department of Information Technology, St. Vincent Pallotti College of Engineering and Technology, Nagpur, India
[3] Department of Computer Science and Engineering, Corporate Institute of Science and Technology, Bhopal, MP, India
[4] Department of Electronics and Communication, Madhyanchal Professional University, Bhopal, MP, India

Abstract. The authentication of users and devices is essential to the security of cyber-physical systems (CPS). But since various networks and devices are interconnected in CPS, they are vulnerable to cyberattacks, which can have detrimental effects on sectors like healthcare, IoT and blockchain technology. This paper highlights the difficulties faced by CPS in the healthcare system and stresses the value of security and privacy in safeguarding private medical information. The resource limitations, security level specifications, and system architecture of CPS-based healthcare systems, conventional security methodologies and cryptography solutions fall short. In order to better preserve and secure CPS in the healthcare industry, this paper investigates the possibilities of machine learning and multi-attribute feature selection. The suggested solution intends to address the drawbacks of traditional privacy preservation techniques and reduce concerns about sensitive information and data leakage. The security of healthcare data in CPS can be improved by utilizing machine learning techniques, which also aids in the creation of strong network security infrastructures for communication in healthcare applications.words.

Keywords: CPS (Cyber-Physical Systems) · Blockchain · Ensemble Learning · IoT · Medical-CPS

1 Introduction

Authentication of users and devices is a core pillar of a cyber-physical system (CPS). The interconnection of heterogeneous networks and devices in a cyber-physical system makes them vulnerable to cyber-attacks. The possibility of cyber-attacks breaks the reachability of cyber-physical systems in health care systems, block-chain development, and the internet of things. Communication and computers have undergone a creative revolution in the last ten years. The Internet has extended across various networks in a wide range of fields, having a substantial influence on all facets of daily life, particularly in the field of medicine. The CPS and MCPS systems have far better social and economic effects. Globally, a number of investments have been made to further this technology [2]. The physical components of the dedicated systems address significant issues, such as dependability, security, and safety requirements because the medical data may be sent across wireless and social networks. Anywhere large-scale networks are installed, security is a serious challenge [3]. Healthcare systems built on CPS deal with data pertaining to people. Even if it was obtained from harmless wearable sensors, major privacy issues might still affect this data. Safety and confidentiality are among the top spaces of concern in CPS-based healthcare applications because the bulk of devices and their connections are wireless. Since CPS-based health care applications directly involve humans, strong and safe data links between medical sensors, controller, sufferers, and caregivers are necessary. People's ability to use CPS-based healthcare apps may be constrained by misuse or privacy issues [4, 5]. Earlier safety and protection measures, such as present cryptographic clarifications, sheltered protocols, and confidentiality assurance, cannot be used in CPS-based medical systems due to supply limitations, refuge level necessities, and system planning. Robust network safety arrangements for short or long range communication are mandatory to reduce the hazards stated above. Wireless networks today have serious security problems that can be fixed, but they don't apply right away to CPS-based healthcare applications. Data leakage and the sensitive nature of the information put the traditional approach to privacy preservation in the healthcare system at risk. The conventional algorithms of privacy preservation face a problem of selection of attributes and information hiding. The development of machine learning makes use of the health care system's cyber-physical systems' ability to protect privacy.

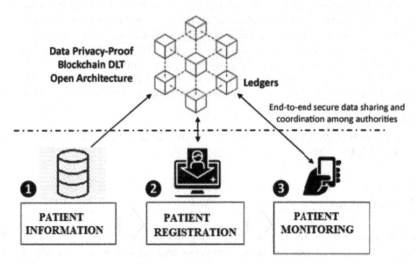

Fig. 1. Blockchain and Healthcare

The selection of features based on multiple criteria improves the idea of health care data security (Fig. 1).

1.1 Ensemble Learning

Gadget mastering ensemble procedures combine the insights from numerous mastering fashions to permit greater unique and higher conclusions. The main assets of errors in getting to know models are noise, variation, and bias. The accuracy and balance of machine studying (ML) algorithms are ensured by way of the ensemble methods utilized in ML, which assist lessen these errors-causing factors. Similar to this, ensemble approaches in machine learning use a number of models and benefit from the combined output, which, when compared to a single model, will undoubtedly be a better choice in terms of prediction accuracy.

1.2 Ensemble Techniques

1.2.1 Bagging or Bootstrap Aggregating

To reduce variance errors in decision trees, the "bagging" or "Bootstrap Aggregating" ensemble method is used. The objective in this case is to create at random replacement samples (subsets of the training data). The subsets are then used to train decision trees or other algorithms. As a result, multiple models are combined, which reduces variance, because the average prediction of multiple models is much more reliable and robust than a single model or decision tree. Using a boosting ensemble approach, data scientists develop subsequent algorithms by matching the residuals of the first boosting algorithm, giving more weight to observations that were incorrectly predicted by the previous model. The first boosting algorithm is trained on the entire data set.

1.2.2 Random Forest Models

The bagging concept can be used with some modification for random forest modifications. A comprehensive selection tree provides access to all available functions while deciding on allocation and selection options. As a result, while bootstrapped samples may not differ nearly as much, entries tend to be split based on identical characteristics for each model. Alternatively, random forest domain models randomly select features and determine where to split. Because each tree is distributed primarily based on different features, random forest shapes contain variance rather than being distributed across comparable features at each node within a year. With a combination of greater mixing, this amount of differentiation creates a greater unique predictor (Fig. 2).

1.2.3 Stacking

Stacking is a way of combining a pair of classification or regression models. There are many approaches to ensemble fashion, the widely recognized fashion being bagging or Boosting. Bagging allows averaging over more than one comparable model with high variance to reduce variance. Scaling builds more than one scaling mode to reduce bias while keeping variance small. Stacking (sometimes known as stacked generalization) is

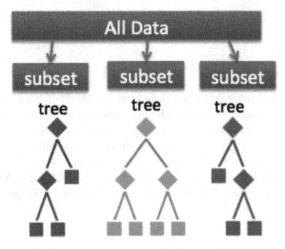

Fig. 2. A random forest extraction from Data Set

a unique paradigm. The purpose of stacking is to examine the state of different models in a single effort. The idea is that a learning problem can be attacked in exclusive ways that can study only part of the problem, but no longer the entire state of the effort. This way you can create more than one separate launcher and use them as intermediate predictions, one prediction for each version you find. Then you add a new model that learns a matching object from intermediate predictions (Fig. 3).

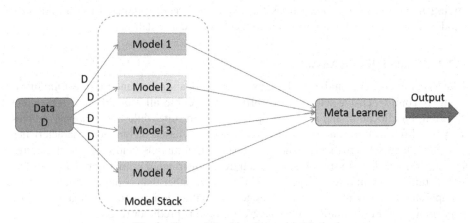

Fig. 3. Flow of Stacking Ensemble Method

1.3 Blockchain Overview

Blockchain is a distributed digital ledger that facilitates decentralized record sharing among peer communities. It was first proposed as a decentralized cryptocurrency by

Nakamoto et al. Blockchain is a group of blocks that can be joined together using times-tamps and cryptographic hashes. Each block is immutable, comfortable, searchable, and transparent. Every time a block is joined to the ending point of the chain, the chain continues to expand, and each fresh block include the hash value of the early block's content. Each node has a public key and a private key that are tied to it. Therefore, the blockchain network uses the concept of an asymmetric secret [12, 13]. Using hash, the blocks are connected to one another. With the use of cryptographic hash characteristics like SHA-256, the hashes are produced. This validates the blocks' immutability and anonymity. The transaction is digitally signed using a private key prior to being broad-cast on a peer-to-peer network. It offers transaction integrity and authentication. The transaction is subsequently broadcast throughout the network and confirmed transac-tions are collected into time-stamped blocks by miners. The network uses the distinctive consensus approach, such as proof of work or evidence of stake, among many others, for settlement in a dispensed network. The blocks are published in a community where they are verified before being included in a chain of blocks. Peer-to-peer acceptance is made possible via blockchain. The three main components of the blockchain generation are distributed ledger, consensus, and cryptography.

1.4 Blockchain and Healthcare Data Security

It's hardly unexpected that the maximum well-liked blockchain healthcare use at the moment is safeguarding medical information. Safety is a good sized trouble inside the healthcare sector. From July 2021 to June 2022, 692 good sized healthcare records breaches have been disclosed. In addition to banking and credit card information, the perpetrators also took health and genomic testing records. Blockchain is a perfect era for data security packages due to its ability to maintain an incorruptible, decentralized and transparent log of all patient facts. In addition, the blockchain is both personal and transparent, incorporating cumbersome and loose protocols to identify each individual, which can protect the sensitivity of medical statistics. The decentralized form of the era also enables free and secure equal sharing of information between patients, doctors and various health experts.

1.5 A Blockchain Model for Health Care

1.5.1 Scalability

A distributed blockchain including documents, photos, or health information would have data storage and throughput restrictions. The allotted community of the fitness care blockchain would no longer be conceivable from a facts storage viewpoint if it were to be constructed after the Bitcoin blockchain due to the fact that every member could have a replica of each health record for everybody within the USA. Due to the dynamic and expansive nature of fitness facts, it might be bandwidth-in depth, wasteful of community assets, and tricky for records throughput to copy all fitness statistics to every network member. Blockchain would want to function a get entry to-control decision maker for health information and data in order for the industry to advantage from it. An ordered series, or a whole listing of all the person's health records and fitness statistics, is the information contained in our proposed medical blockchain. The index is similar to a library's correspondence catalog. The location of the eBook and its statistics are both listed in the card catalog. The same concepts could practice to the fitness blockchain (Fig. 4).

Fig. 4. Data Lake

1.5.2   Access Security and Data Privacy

The handler would be in whole control of his data and would have full access to it. The operator would choice that can query and write data to his blockchain and establish a set of access permissions. The user ought to check who has get entry to his blockchain the usage of a cell dashboard application. Additionally, the handler would be able to see a record of who accessed their blockchain, as well as when and what information was accessed. The user would be able to grant and cancel access authorizations to some person with an exclusive identity using the same dashboard. The flexibility of access control permissions would allow them to manage more situations than "all-or-nothing" permits. The user defines precise and comprehensive processes for who has access, authorized access time, and specific categories of data that can be retrieved. The user has the option to change access rights at any time. Only the user can change the access control restrictions, which would be securely stored on the blockchain. It creates a

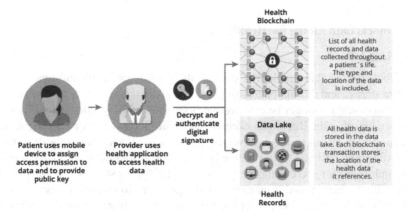

Fig. 5. Data flow in health care system

transparent environment and gives the user full control over what facts are collected and how they are shared (Fig. 5).

2 Literature Survey

Author [1] uses IoT architecture in smart healthcare in this study. This algorithm predicts appropriate medications for patients using clustering and machine learning (ML) techniques. Spark is used to run data collected initially on recycled servers. Second, clusters of significant features are created using a clustering algorithm (K-means) for disease-based classification. Finally, predictive methods such as Naive Bayes and Random Forest are used to group the most appropriate medications for patients. Studies were conducted on two common Unique Customer Identifier (UCI) machine learning datasets. Patient clusters are created using the k-means clustering technique.

The author [2] in suggest a privacy-preserving method for protecting medical plaintext data against unauthorized access via holomorphic encryption. Secret sharing spreads calculations to a number of effective nodes at the control and secretes all mathematics operations to avoid unreliable cloud servers from improve the state taken on the encipher patient data. In-depth comparisons and contrasts are made between the suggested plan and recent research publications.

The author [3] This paper's major goal is to shed light on blockchain technology's potential applications for healthcare security, privacy protection, and future research paths. In order to provide problems and comparisons between different published works in the tract of blockchain for health care, we have identified and analyzed the most recent research papers and literature. With the use of blockchain technology, patients are able to own their own data.

The author [4] proposed a SC-UCSSO -user-controlled single sign-on for telemedicine structures based on smartcards that not only achieves confidentiality but then also increases security equated to earlier systems that were demonstrated with BAN logic and AVISPA (Automated Validation of Internet Security Protocols and Applications). Additionally, we offered a performance analysis and demonstrated how the suggested scheme outperformed earlier schemes that were evaluated and how the mathematical complexity of the handler in the suggested scheme had nothing to do with the quantity of servers.

According to author [5] the current level of security in cryptography is dictated by how well random number generation has improved. They suggest a cutting-edge defense against a replay assault that takes advantage of the timestamp. Using the Elliptic Curve Discrete Logarithmic Problem (ECDLP), we provide strong forward security that makes it difficult to understand the adversary's security settings.

The approach proposed by the author [6] uses authority servers to support healthcare workers in tracking caregivers who stop contact tracing or are unable to do so. As computing devices have access to more meaningful data and require less data collection, businesses, homes and offices can now participate as locations in contact tracing. In addition, by providing a point of contact for nearby power calculation strategies, the proposed technique reduces the total energy consumption of end users by up to 97%.

The author [7] uses the RDT method is employed in this research study to overcome the aforementioned problems. A more complicated version of the Bayes classification technique is the RDT. RDT outperforms other approaches in terms of safeguarding current knowledge and avoiding information loss. A system dataset of patients with diabetes was created in order to validate the performance of RDT. With little calculation time and information loss, the RDT algorithm successfully conserved and recovered the data.

In an effort to increase the safety and confidentiality of IoT connections in midst of massive data, the author [8] established server privacy and developed exclusive signs using device attributes. These sorts may remain the same dependent on the user, however once the device talks; identification is changed to protect privacy. The Attribute Management System (AMS), a dedicated server, is used to allocate IDs based on the properties of IoT devices.

The protocol's implementation is based on interconnected information, which enables the huge information involved in the accidents to be meaningfully characterized and coupled with applicable educational data sources, on which the author [9] concentrated. The k-means data sets that the procedure delivers nonetheless contain crucial information, enabling common data investigation and algebraic analysis tasks. The suggested procedure forbids the re-identification of persons using their sensitive information, according to the systematic and experiential study. Implementing the planned procedure would make use of linked data and multiple linked data platform instances.

The author's [10] focused on current state of confidentiality preservation clarifications in edge healthcare and Internet of Things claims. It defines the collective approaches academics take to include privacy in their medical solutions. The researchers also discourse these result shortcomings in positions of their effectiveness, practical sustainability & complexity. The assessment and discussion of the challenges that must be addressed in order to safeguard privacy in edge healthcare and IoT solutions for future applications concludes the article.

The author [11] employed potentially sensitive information may be present in data from sectors like banking and healthcare that, if not adequately cleansed, could end up in the public domain. Federated learning (Fed ML), a newly created DML-distributed machine learning technique, seeks to guarantee confidentiality by provision of the learning of a machine-learning model to the data clutch. Research suggests that a number of attack strategies, including membership inference, can be used to retrieve private data by exploiting the flaws in ML models and the coordinating servers. Fed ML must therefore take further measures to guarantee data privacy. This paper put forth the DISTPAB distributed perturbation approach. Consequently, distributed machine learning may become private.

SUSI-Single User Sign-In protocol, developed by the author [12] of this study, guarantees privacy preservation. A shared session-key may be negotiated in order to encrypt or decode highly sensitive information during the authentication process. In order to achieve important agreement qualities like sufficient common confirmation and assured session key agreement, suggested system architecture is integrated into the hectic map. The SUSI is an recommended scheme can accomplish more than only the security aspects of the protocol called AKA, such as effective shared validation, according to the security analysis.

In healthcare communication, the author [13] emphasized the need of sensitively interpreting and allocating information to assist patients and to inform the public. ML-Machine Learning has demonstrated application in medical system due to its capabilities for managing complex dialogues and informal elasticity. In this subject analysis, research focused on how using ML-Machine Learning/AI in healthcare communication might benefit patients. This includes the COVID-19 health education, cancer treatment, and health imaging.

[14] In this privacy preservation idea transforms the outdated data analysis methods into a scattered and non-reusable form in order to minimize the leakage of patients' health information. The researchers also created a risk-based privacy quantification framework to complement existing privacy quantification methods to evaluate the effectiveness of DnD-based privacy preservation.

3   Problem Identification

The protection of patient data should come first. By using current security standards and validation techniques, the patient data must be completely protected, encrypted, and secured in applications. These security issues were carefully examined for MCPS as a whole. Cloud-based healthcare systems face significant challenges from security concerns such as the illegal use of data and the manipulation of patients' sensitive cloud data. As a result, there are a variety of security requirements that MCPS and cloud-based healthcare systems must adhere to.

Authentication: Patients, healthcare professionals, and other users' identities must be verified using a reliable cryptographic method.

Authorization: After authentication, this is the second prerequisite that assures that users of the system will have access to resources, be granted authorization, and be given priority access. Users are given varying levels of access depending on the privilege.

Non-repudiation: To confirm that the sender of this communication has actually transmitted it, a cryptographic technique has been used. A digital signature, encryption, and timestamps may be used to ensure the patient in a medical system and to ensure the patient's legitimacy and non-repudiation. Integrity and Confidentiality: The integrity ensures the integrity of the communication received. We can say that the healthcare system has not modified any patient data.

4   Objectives

To ensure that each type of privacy preservation can be categorized into one of the models and that the proper actions can be taken to safeguard the whole system, the MCPS Cyber Security Framework was introduced. This enhances the security features of MCPS. In terms of the industry, several cybersecurity frameworks have previously been proposed. The quantitative evaluation of the security frameworks, however, was never emphasized in many of the cybersecurity frameworks that had previously been proposed. The survey of cyber-physical systems uses the authentication process and sets the following objectives:

- To perform privacy preservation analysis behavioral modelling of known data leakage in MCPS.
- To design and develop key management and key exchange mechanism using multi-attribute ensemble classifier for MCPS use cases.
- To propose lightweight MIE algorithm for identified assets.
- To design framework and compare the outcomes which state of arts in order to validate the findings.

5   Proposed Methodology

The proposed methodology of MCPS applies the process of authentication to overcome the limitation of data integrity and continentality. The proposed method uses multi-attribute ensemble approach for key authentication. The ensemble classifier several characteristics can affect how the key generation scheme is built. It is advisable to identify every aspect that affects the plan in detail and assess the usefulness or utility of each one. An additional key used in the creation of authentication keys. Before the system ever starts, the sender and recipient pre-share this specific key. The current authentication key for the channel (Fig. 6).

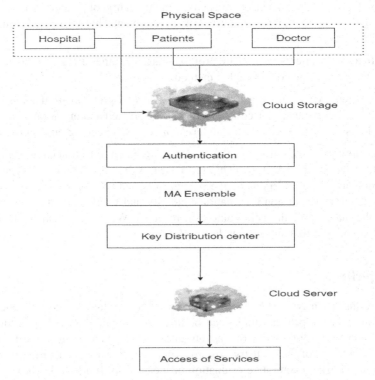

Fig. 6. Proposed model of MCPS based on authentication approach

To achieve the desired goals, following steps will be performed:

1. A comprehensive literature survey of the MCPS related security attacks and prevention methods.
2. Analyzed the various security protocols used in MCPS for network layer.
3. Analysis of various packet-based attacks over the network layer.
4. Analysis of machine learning algorithm used in MCPS security.
5. Simulation of the existing methods.
6. Enhancement of existing security protocol with MA ensemble classifier.
7. Performance analysis of proposed algorithm and performance various securities threats and measure the robustness of algorithm.

6 Integration of Blockchain, Ensemble Learning, and User-Controlled Single Sign-On Uniquely Addresses the Challenges Posed by Medical Cyber-Physical Systems

Incorporating blockchain, ensemble learning, and user-controlled single sign-on (SSO) can provide a singular and all-encompassing solution to the issues raised by medical cyber-physical systems. Let's examine how each of these technologies helps to address the issues.

6.1 Blockchain

Sensitive medical data can be managed, shared, and stored in a decentralized and secured manner thanks to blockchain technology. The following advantages of blockchain are relevant to medical cyber-physical systems, where data confidentiality and integrity are crucial.

6.2 Data Integrity

Medical data is kept accurate and tamper-proof because to the immutable and transparent properties of blockchain. This is essential for preserving the accuracy of patient records, treatment regimens, and information on medical devices.

6.3 Security

The consensus methods and cryptographic concepts used by blockchains improve the security of medical data. Unauthorized entry, data breaches, and unauthorized modifications can all be avoided.

6.4 Auditability

The blockchain allows for the auditing and tracing of every transaction and change made to the medical data, assuring accountability and compliance with rules like HIPAA.

6.5 Ensemble Learning

To improve the overall quality and dependability of predictions, ensemble learning combines the predictions of various machine learning model. The following benefits of ensemble learning are applicable to medical cyber-physical systems:

6.5.1 Enhanced Accuracy

For diagnosis and treatment choices, medical systems require precise predictions. The possibility of inaccurate predictions from individual models is reduced with the aid of ensemble approaches.

6.5.2 Robustness

Ensemble learning can handle uncertainties and changes in medical data by mixing various models, making the system more resilient to various conditions.

6.5.3 Risk Assessment

In order to help in the early detection and prevention of medical concerns, ensemble learning can offer patients more precise risk evaluations.

7 User-Controlled Single Sign-On (SSO)

Patients and medical professionals are given more control over their identities and access to medical data thanks to user-controlled SSO. Within the context of medical cyber-physical systems, it provides the following advantages:

Predictive Accuracy: When combined with trustworthy and secure data from blockchain, ensemble learning's better prediction accuracy leads to more successful diagnostic and therapeutic outcomes.

Interoperability: The decentralized ledger of a blockchain can act as a platform for data exchange across various medical systems, promoting interoperability while upholding security.

Auditability and Accountability: The transparency and auditability of blockchain technology makes it easier to keep track of all data interactions, and user-controlled SSO guarantees that only authorized users have access to the data.

8 Expected Outcomes of the Proposed Work

The multi-attribute ensemble technique for MCPS serves as the foundation for the key authentication design. Lowers the chance of data leaking and gives patients and clinicians a totally secure information route. The following results are anticipated:

1. Increased resistance to data leaking.

2. Achieving the ideal forward secrecy, which is difficult to achieve with only traditional symmetric algorithms?
3. Attribute-key validation must be provided.
4. The way social insurance is communicated to patients has improved because to the advanced use of innovation in medical technologies.
5. The architecture was developed with the numerous security concerns that MCPS encounters in mind.
6. The suggested framework uses individual models to handle the issues raised above, and it is anticipated that the framework will cover more security problems.

9 Result and Discussion

On this hypothetical example, four ensembles getting to know methods (Random wooded area, Gradient Boosting, AdaBoost, and Stacking) had been implemented to a fitness care dataset with multiple attributes.

The performance of each method become evaluated the usage of not unusual assessment metrics:

Accuracy, Precision, recollect, F1 rating, and vicinity below the Receiver operating feature Curve (AUC-ROC). The values in the table constitute the overall performance accomplished by means of each ensemble approach at the unique fitness care undertaking.

Accuracy: The overall accuracy of the version in making accurate predictions.

Precision: The percentage of genuine high-quality predictions amongst all effective predictions.

ReCall: The proportion of real wonderful predictions amongst all real nice times.

F1 Rating: The harmonic mean of precision and consider, representing the balance among the 2 metrics.

AUC-ROC: The location below the Receiver working function Curve, a degree of the version's potential to discriminate between tremendous and negative instances (Table 1 and Fig. 7).

Table 1. Comparision of Ensemble methods on Health Care Data

Ensemble Method	Accuracy	Precision	Recall	F1 Score	AUC-ROC
Random Forest	0.853	0.836	0.872	0.853	0.914
Gradient Boosting	0.864	0.844	0.884	0.866	0.922
AdaBoost	0.833	0.813	0.851	0.831	0.902
Stacking	0.878	0.866	0.894	0.878	0.928

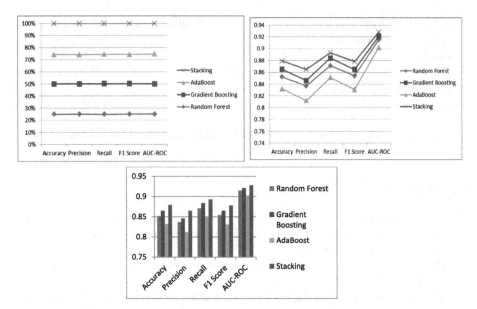

Fig. 7. Comparision of Ensemble methods on Health Care Data

1. The precision (0.866), accuracy (0.878), recall (0.894), F1 score (0.878), and AUC-ROC (0.928) values are all highest for the Stacking ensemble approach.
2. With accuracy of 0.866 and good values for F1 score, recall, precision and AUC-ROC, gradient boosting also performs well across all metrics.
3. When compared to stacking and gradient boosting, Random Forest and AdaBoost perform slightly worse due to differences in accuracy, AUC-ROC, F1 score precision & recall.

   These outcomes suggest that the Stacking ensemble method appears to be the most effective among the options provided, followed closely by Gradient Boosting.

10   Conclusion

From the above consequences the findings show that ensemble studying can significantly increase the reliability and accuracy of predictive fashions used in the healthcare enterprise. With an accuracy of zero.878, precision of zero.866, recall of zero.894, F1 rating of zero.878, and AUC-ROC of zero.928, stacking outperformed all different ensemble strategies tested. This shows that merging several fashions can efficaciously perceive numerous styles and relationships inside the statistics, generating predictions with higher degree of accuracy.

Bibliography

1. Aldabbas, H., Albabish, D., Khatatneh, K., Amin, R.: An architecture of IoT-aware healthcare smart system by leveraging machine learning. Int. Arab J. Inf. Technol. **19**(2), 160–172 (2022)
2. Salim, M.M., Kim, I., Doniyor, U., Lee, C., Park, J.H.: Homomorphic encryption based privacy-preservation for IOMT. Appl. Sci. **11**(18), 8757 (2021)
3. Raghav, N., Bhola, A.: Blockchain based privacy preservation in healthcare: a recent trends and challenges. Psychol. Educ. J **58**, 5315–5324 (2021)
4. Lin, T.-W., Hsu, C.-L., Le, T.-V., Chung-Fu, L., Huang, B.-Y.: A smartcard-based user-controlled single sign-on for privacy preservation in 5G-IoT telemedicine systems. Sensors **21**(8), 2880 (2021)
5. Kishore, P., Barisal, S.K., Kumar, K.V., Mohapatra, D.P.: Security improvement and privacy preservation in e-health. In: IEEE International Conference on Communications, ICC 2021, pp. 1–6. IEEE (2021)
6. Alsahli, M.A., Alsanad, A., Hassan, M.M., Gumaei, A.: Privacy preservation of user identity in contact tracing for COVID-19-like pandemics using edge computing. IEEE Access **9**, 125065–125079 (2021)
7. Sharif, M.H.U.: Privacy preservation of medical data using random decision tree. Int. J. Res. Educ. Sci. Meth. **9**, 1674–1679 (2021)
8. DivyaKeerthi, S., Ashokkumar, K., Sangeetha, S.K.B., Gayathri, S., Kamala, K.: IoT-enabled infrastructure privacy preservation in big data. Eur. J. Mol. Clin. Med. **8**(2), 724–731 (2021)
9. Rodriguez-Garcia, M., Balderas, A., Dodero, J.M.: Privacy preservation and analytical utility of e-learning data mashups in the web of data. Appl. Sci. **11**(18), 8506 (2021)
10. Almusallam, N., Alabdulatif, A., Alarfaj, F.: Analysis of privacy-preserving edge computing and internet of things models in healthcare domain. Comput. Math. Meth. Med. **2021**, 1–6 (2021)
11. Chamikara, M.A., Pathum, P.B., Khalil, I., Liu, D., Camtepe, S.: Privacy preserving distributed machine learning with federated learning. Comput. Commun. **171**, 112–125 (2021)
12. Deebak, B.D., Al-Turjman, F., Nayyar, A.: Chaotic-map based authenticated security framework with privacy preservation for remote point-of-care. Multimedia Tools Appl. **80**, 17103–17128 (2021)
13. Siddique, S., Chow, J.C.L.: Machine learning in healthcare communication. Encyclopedia **1**(1), 220–239 (2021)
14. Aqueveque, P., Gómez, B., Williams, P.A.H., Li, Z.: A novel privacy preservation and quantification methodology for implementing home-care-oriented movement analysis systems. Sensors **22**(13), 4677 (2022)
15. Wu, Y., Dai, H.-N., Wang, H., Choo, K.-K.R.: Blockchain-based privacy preservation for 5G-enabled drone communications. IEEE Netw. **35**(1), 50–56 (2021)
16. Truonga, N., Suna, K., Wanga, S., Guittona, F., Guoa, YiKe.: Privacy preservation in federated learning: insights from the GDPR perspective. Comput. Secur. **110**, 102402 (2021)
17. Hasanova, H., Tufail, M., Baek, U.-J., Park, J.-T., Kim, M.-S.: A novel blockchain-enabled heart disease prediction mechanism using machine learning. Comput. Electr. Eng. **101**, 108086 (2022)
18. Ahmed, I., Zhang, Y., Jeon, G., Lin, W., Khosravi, M.R., Qi, L.: A blockchain-and artificial intelligence-enabled smart IoT framework for sustainable city. Int. J. Intell. Syst. **37**(9), 6493–6507 (2022)
19. Mahzabin, R., Sifat, F.H., Anjum, S., Nayan, A.-A., Kibria, M.G.: Blockchain associated machine learning and IoT based hypoglycemia detection system with auto-injection feature. arXiv preprint arXiv:2208.02222 (2022)

20. Kaushik, K., Kumar, A.: Demystifying quantum blockchain for healthcare. Secur. Priv. **6**, e284 (2022)
21. Khan, A.A., et al.: Healthcare ledger management: a blockchain and machine learning-enabled novel and secure architecture for medical industry. Hum, Centric Comput. Inf. Sci. **12**, 1–14 (2022)
22. Abbas, A.F., Qureshi, N.A., Khan, N., Chandio, R., Ali, J.: The blockchain technologies in healthcare: prospects, obstacles, and future recommendations; lessons learned from digitalization. Int. J. Online Biomed. Eng. **18**(9), 144–159 (2022)
23. AlGhamdi, R., Alassafi, M.O., Alshdadi, A.A., Dessouky, M.M., Ramdan, R.A., Aboshosha, B.W.: Developing trusted IoT healthcare information-based AI and blockchain. Processes **11**(1), 34 (2022)
24. Lakhan, A., et al.: Federated-learning based privacy preservation and fraud-enabled blockchain IoMT system for healthcare. IEEE J. Biomed. Health Inf. **27**, 664–672 (2022)
25. Rahmadika, S., Astillo, P.V., Choudhary, G., Duguma, D.G., Sharma, V., You, I.: Blockchain-based privacy preservation scheme for misbehavior detection in lightweight IoMT devices. IEEE J. Biomed. Health Inf. **27**, 710–721 (2022)
26. Verma, G.: Blockchain-based privacy preservation framework for healthcare data in cloud environment. J. Exp. Theoret. Artif. Intell., 1–14 (2022)
27. Kumar, S., Chaube, M.K., Nenavath, S.N., Gupta, S.K., Tetarave, S.K.: Privacy preservation and security challenges: a new frontier multimodal machine learning research. Int. J. Sensor Netw. **39**(4), 227–245 (2022)
28. Ch, R., Srivastava, G., Nagasree, Y.L.V., Ponugumati, A., Ramachandran, S.: Robust cyber-physical system enabled smart healthcare unit using blockchain technology. Electronics **11**(19), 3070 (2022)
29. Ashraf, E., Areed, N.F.F., Salem, H., Abdelhay, E.H., Farouk, A.: Fidchain: Federated intrusion detection system for blockchain-enabled IoT healthcare applications. Healthcare **10**(6), 1110 (2022)
30. Puri, G.D., Haritha, D.: Improving privacy preservation approach for healthcare data using frequency distribution of delicate information. Int. J. Adv. Comput. Sci. Appl. **13**(9) (2022)

Visual Question Answering System for Skeletal Images Based on Feature Extraction Using Faster RCNN and Kai-Bi-LSTM Techniques

Y. I. Jinesh Melvin[✉], Sushopti Gawade, and Mukesh Shrimali

Department of Computer Engineering, Pacific Academy of Higher Education and Research University, Pacific Hills, Pratapnagar Extn., Airport Road, Udaipur, Debari, India
`yijmelvin@mes.ac.in`

Abstract. The human life cycle is becoming more intelligent in the present era of technology, and it is expanding quickly in many areas, particularly in healthcare. In The HealthCare industry, we can see lots of significant transformation with the help of different cutting-edge technologies such as telemedicine, electronic medical records, drone technology, digital tools, and Artificial Intelligence. The main goals of AI are to complement medical expertise and enhance patient interaction. Most of the patients may not be aware of their health while revealing imaginary reports. Answering questions from visual reports is very challenging for doctors and patients. So the design of a VQA (Visual Question Answering) system for skeletal images based on feature extraction methods comes into play for the Healthcare realm to solve the complex problems against the visual images for users' queries. In fact, it is a challenging task as it constrains the interaction and complementation of both image feature extraction and text feature extraction. This VQA system that can comprehend medical images may also aid in clinical decision-making, clinical education, and patient health literacy. Clinical questions are more challenging, but due to the importance of health and safety, answers must be highly accurate. Different techniques were used in this design to extract and categorize the textual and visual data. Faster R-CNN and Kai-Bi-LSTM are the design models for feature extraction that are suggested here. Deep Conversational neural networks are used in image feature extraction to find things. In order to combine past and feature context information, the BiLSTM neural network is made up of LSTM units that function in both directions. In order to forecast precise responses for given users' inquiries for the image that they placed into the system, we combine the two methodologies mentioned above and classify.

Keywords: VQA · Faster-RCNN · BiLSTM · Classification · Visual Medical Images

1 Introduction

The primary objective of Visual Question Answering (VQA) on skeletal images is to develop models that can answer questions in natural language that are important for diagnosing medical images. It can aid people in the interpretation of their medical images and

S. Ponnusamy and V. R. Bora (Eds.): AIBTR 2023, CCIS 1987, pp. 87–101, 2024.
https://doi.org/10.1007/978-3-031-49454-3_6

offer significant new insights to medical experts. To aid clinicians, patients, and doctors, many companies have created diverse software. Researchers are also eager to advance technologically-assisted innovative methods that will benefit society. Patients struggle with recognizing their physical and mental health issues. Communication between the doctor and the patient is crucial for learning precise information about the body and health. When responding to health issues, doctors or clinicians may or may not use phrases that patients can understand. It takes a variety of skills, including item localization, attribute identification, scene comprehension, reasoning, counting, and more, to provide accurate answers to these questions. However, for supervised learning algorithms to perform well, huge labeled datasets are necessary. As a result, systems for visual question-answering on medical images have been proposed in this work using B12 FRCNN (Faster Region-based Convolutional Neural Networks) and Kai-Bi-LSTM (Kaiming Bidirectional Long short-term Memory).

2   Related Work

The inability to generate an accurate, concise description of a patient's state that is comparable to a clinician's diagnosis is a significant drawback of Complementary diagnosis technology based on the analysis of a single type of medical imaging. This promise is realized by the VQA-Med system. Despite having a large amount of training data support, the present VQA-Med datasets frequently have issues; as a result, this is an area that has to be improved. This is due to the fact that inaccurate data can make classification errors worse, even when they are backed by a large amount of training data. VQA-Med is important for scientific research.

Initially, this field is still in its early stages, and there are numerous unexplored technologies. Additionally, adapting the model data is essential due to the absence of standardized data sources. This study establishes the accessibility of the VQA-Med system for patient consultations and medical research. It builds upon a range of suggested solutions that form the foundational framework for VQA-Med as a research model. Challenges include the specialized processing of medical terminology within medical texts and images, the complexities of integrating multi-modal features across different levels of medical data, and the often overlooked interaction between questions and the visual data extracted from textual semantics.

Shengyan Liu et al. [1] developed a brand-new bi-branched Model for Medical Visual Question Answering (BPI-MVQA) based on Parallel Networks and Image Retrieval. A transformer architecture based on a parallel network, was used in the first iteration of BPI-MVQA to provide complementary advantages in the extraction of spatial and image sequence information. Multi-head self-attention was used to implicitly combine multi-modal properties. In the second branch, text labels were produced using the second branch's similarity of picture features produced by the VGG16 network. On three VQA-Med datasets, the BPI-MVQA model generated ground-breaking results.

In this study, a novel bi-branched model (BPI-MVQA) [1] based on parallel networks and image retrieval was proposed for addressing medical visual questions. When extracting spatial and image sequence features, the first branch of BPI-MVQA uses a transformer structure based on a parallel network to obtain complementary advantages. The multi-head self-attention mechanism enables the implicit fusion of multi-modal properties. In the second branch, the similarity of the visual attributes the VGG16 network has gathered is extracted to create text labels.

Lubna A. et al.'s research on the visual question-answering for skeletal images in the ImageCLEF 2019 medical VQA dataset was covered in [2]. The approach took into account the difficulty of replying to modality-based queries for medical images such as X-rays, Computed Tomography (CT), Ultrasound (US), Magnetic Resonance Imaging (MRI), etc. The approach used in this instance entailed classifying the input image according to its modality class using a convolutional neural network (CNN), and then delivering the solution based on the CNN output. The testing accuracy of the model was 83.8%, which was comparable to methods used at the time.

Fazal Muhammad et al. [3] adopted reverse frequency allocation (RFA). Decoupled DL-UL association (De-DUA) was also emphasized in addition to coupled DL-UL association (Co-DUA). In De-DUA, a randomly selected user was connected to the BSs of two separate tiers, one in the DL direction and the other in the UL direction. The findings showed that De-DUA with RFA employment outperforms Co-DUA in terms of coverage performance.

Considering the difficulties being performed, Dhruv Sharma et al. [4] designed Med-FuseNet, an attention-based multimodal deep learning network, for VQA on medical images. MedFuseNet divided the issue statement into simpler tasks and predicted the solution in an effort to maximize learning with the least amount of complexity. The categories and the generation of two different answer prediction classifications were addressed. The trials showed that MedFuseNet outperformed cutting-edge VQA techniques and that visualization of the attention-grabbing content highlighted the model's expected outcomes' interpretability.

Fuji Ren et al. [5] designed a model called CGMVQA (Classification and Generative Model for Medical Visual Question Answering) that contains categorization and answer generating skills in order to divide this substantial task into a number of smaller ones. Texts were determined to be tokenized, and image data was included. The pretrained ResNet152 was used to merge three distinct embedding types and extract picture features to deal with texts. The model produced cutting-edge outcomes in the ImageCLEF 2019 VQA-Med data set, with classification accuracy of 0.640, word matching of 0.659, and semantic similarity of 0.678. It was suggested that the CGMVQA might aid physicians in clinical analysis and diagnosis and be successful in resolving medical visual questions.

Rahhal, Mohamad Mahmoud AI [6] the method described in this article uses the Vision Transformer (ViT) model to extract visual information and is built on a transformer encoder-decoder structure. This system then combines the created textual and visual representations, feeding them through a multi-modal decoder to create the answer in an autoregressive manner. Use the radiological imaging datasets from VQA-RAD and PathVQA to verify the suggested model. By posing questions about specific characteristics of the image, visual question answering (VQA), a recent advancement in machine vision, seeks to improve picture captioning [7]. Transformers have showcased their capacity to grasp the relationships among sequence elements, unlike Recurrent Neural Networks (RNNs), which iteratively handle sequence components and consider only the present context. Transformer architectures can establish far-reaching connections by focusing on entire sequences. In particular, the model that is most frequently used to represent textual data is the transformers' bidirectional encoder representation (BERT) [8]. BERT is a language model that builds context-sensitive representations of each word in a phrase using large-scale unsupervised corpora and a bidirectional attention mechanism.

Both local features and full-scale picture features can be extracted; we advise using a parallel structure based on ResNet152 [9, 10] and Gate Recurrent Unit (GRU) [11]. Images collected in different dimensions must have their spatial feature data retained. The sequence feature information of the original three-channel images is then preserved before being converted into single-channel grayscale images and transmitted into the stacked GRU network. The output of the features from the GRU network and the features created from each layer of ResNet152 are combined in order to create complete features for the images.

The primary component of the multi-classification model we use is the transformer structure model. By comprehending complicated biomedical literature using the biomedical corpus on PubMed, Biobert [12] outperforms Bidirectional Encoder Representations from Transformers (Bert) [13] in several biomedical text mining tasks and for biomedical data training. Instead of using the conventional Bert model input, we use the concatenated picture features and question features as the transformer's input and take advantage of their varied qualities. The model innovates and improves outcomes through the multi-head self-attention process, which integrates the input properties.

A lot of innovative methods for achieving VQA objectives have emerged as a result of the development of VQA-Med. The field of VQA-Med can also benefit from these methods. The feature extractor is frequently a classical convolution neural network (CNN) pre-trained on ImageNet, and the picture feature extractor is frequently a recurrent neural network (RNN) or a model of transformer structure. The multi-modal factorized bilinear pooling model (MFB) is a deep network model that Peng et al. [14] proposed based on ResNet152 and LSTM.

The Zhejiang University team won first place in the ImageCLEF2019 VQA-Med assignment the year after thanks to their [15] creative model, which could extract question characteristics using Bert and picture attributes from the middle layer of VGG16. A modular pipeline architecture utilizing transfer learning and multitask learning was introduced by Kornuta et al. [16]. In order to succeed on the ImageCLEF2021 VQAMed test, Liao et al. [17] applied the Skeleton-based Sentence Mapping (SSM) knowledge inference methodology. Al-Sadi et al.'s [18] second-place showing on the ImageCLEF2021 VQA-Med exam was achieved by successfully utilizing data augmentation. In order to automatically develop suitable reasoning techniques for a variety of Med-VQA difficulties, Zhang et al. [19] suggested a novel conditional reasoning framework for Med-VQA. The insights of the literature review mentioned in figure [1].

2.1 Summary of Literature Survey

Several models were preserved from other research, and the Classification and generation model, which relied upon Image CLEF 2019 datasets, is an efficient medical visual question-answering system. In the final stages of the current literature survey, insights include results and limitations in which accuracy was exhibited, along with types of inputs in terms of questions and the feature extraction of images and text with a classification algorithm (Fig. 1).

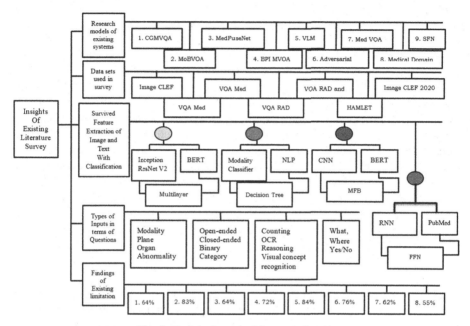

Fig. 1. Insight from the Literature Survey

3   Area of Improvement

The existing research methodologies have some limitations which are identified in this paper. Some of them are to extract local regional vectors for local areas, the current VQA models use CNN. The feature vectors for the related question are encoded using LSTM. When the response consists of two neighboring local regions in the image and the question being asked is a complex sentence, the answer produced by these attention mechanisms is not entirely accurate. There aren't enough publicly accessible, well-annotated datasets for the Med-VQA system's training and evaluation. The computer-aided diagnosis technology currently in use is often focused on a single ailment. Its inability to produce a complex, Comprehensive assessment of a patient's state similar to a Physician's assessment is a key limitation of auxiliary diagnosis technology based on the analysis of a single type of medical imaging. For such data, the existing approach cannot handle complex data, and vector formation yields the poorest results. The existing approach just uses the prior contextual information from the query and does not use the subsequent contextual information. When extracting the question feature, it leads to errors.

4   Identification of Research Gap

There have been several innovative methods for VQA tasks developed as a result of the highly interesting design problem of VQA-Med. The VQA-Med field can also use these strategies. Although it has not yet been fully developed, the visual question answering in the medical sector (VQA-Med) technology offers a lot of potential in medical applications. Prior to VQA-Med, there was a question-and-answer (QA) system for medicine that was mostly used for databases, other technologies, and information retrieval. The innovative, carefully thought-out objectives of the proposed research project create the VQA system for a better society. To propose an ideal approach for extracting image and text features from radiology images for the VQA system that provides high accuracy and performs better than the current one. Using the Selective Search algorithm, it generates 2,000 region ideas from the provided images. The second module takes a feature vector of length 4,096 from each region proposal and shrinks it to a predetermined fixed size. A pre-trained SVM algorithm allocates the region suggestion to the background or one of the object classes in the third module. The Kaiming initialization method causes enormously deep models (>30 layers) to converge by delicately modeling ReLU (Rectified Linear Unit) non-linearity for textual feature extraction. The desired layer-by-layer mean and variance for the weight distribution following ReLU should be somewhat higher than 1. With a mean of 0 and a variance of 1, we initialize weight using a normal distribution.

In a technically sophisticated society, the automated VQA medical dominance system is highly difficult to operate, and the user needs correct responses to questions regarding the images. Because it's all about people's health, it's a very arduous task. Regarding the human medical system, sufficient clarity of communication is required. To propose an automated system for answering the question asked by the user in the medical images. There are many medical terms, which make it very difficult for users to understand. The creation of a dictionary word is a necessary aspect of the VQA system. So, this system will propose a novel algorithm for dictionary creation for image and Question-Answer (QA) pairs. The system can be improved by comparing many models with various datasets that plot better model performance. To compare the effectiveness of the suggested methodology with currently used methods and to demonstrate the novelty of the suggested method.

5   Proposed Research Methodology System Design

When organizing a task known as "visual question answering," the computer is given an image and a relevant question as input, and the output is a suitable solution to the query. One of the long-standing objectives of AI research is to create machines that can comprehend visual content and respond to queries just like humans. Visual question answering (VQA) has grown in popularity as a subject of study recently. A clinical query is accompanied by a radiological image within the scope of medical visual question answering (Med-VQA), and the objective is to develop a system that can accurately respond to the question based on the visual information of the image.

The proposed system uses a novel classifier to help patients. The following steps are carried out in the proposed system. The proposed system has two phases, the training phase and the testing phase. In the training phase, the radiology images with question-answer pairs are taken as input. The image feature is extracted by using the Proposed Block_12_add Faster R-CNN (B12-FRCNN) algorithm. The existing FRCNN algorithm uses "activation_40_relu" as a feature layer, which has a gradient vanishing problem. So the feature layer of FRCNN is modified with the "block_12_add" layer. The selection of the optimal feature extraction layer needs to be empirically analyzed.

Then the Question-Answer (QA) pair is taken. The preprocessing is done for both the question and the answer. First, the question text is taken. The whole text is split into individual words. Then Stop Word Removal is carried out to eliminate the words that frequently appear. Words such as "a", "an", and "the" do not provide any meaning to the text, but appear often. Hence, those words are considered stop words, and they have been removed. Then stemming is carried out. In the computational process of stemming, affixes from confounded words are shortened to reveal the root. In other words, it refers to chopping off a word's ending and leaving only the base. Condensing words with diverse suffixes under a single root word is what this signifies. For instance, the term "connection" can be combined with other words like "connective" and "connected" to form the word "connect". To increase computation efficiency, text stemmers aim to reduce the size of the index. The question's keywords are extracted following preprocessing. A group of one or more words that are thought to be extremely significant constitutes a keyword. The method of extracting pertinent information from the text is known as keyword extraction. And text-only splitting is carried out for the response.

The output from the previous step is in the form of strings and is converted into a numerical format for the purpose of effective classification. Such conversion of textual data into numbers is based on the hypothesis of word representation. This strategy in our proposed work is done by using LogishBERT. Bidirectional Encoder Representations from Transformers (BERT) [8] is a pre-trained model composed of an encoder component of a bidirectional transformer that converts an input string or input sentence pair into word embedding. This pre-trained model uses the GELU activation function in the fully connected layer. After this layer's output is transformed into vocabulary, a softmax function is used to forecast the hidden word. The GELU activation is unable to handle complex data; for such data, the vector formation provides the least results. In order to overcome this drawback, a Logarithmic Swish activation function is used in the general BERT, and the proposed system is called LogishBERT. The output of this LogishBERT is numerical data and is called a score value.

Once the word embedding is done, the extracted radiology image feature and the score value of the question and answer text are given to train the classifier. Our proposed work utilizes a Kai-Bi-LSTM classifier for answer prediction. A sequence processing model called Bidirectional LSTM, or BiLSTM, consists of two LSTMs. One receives input going forward, and the other goes backward. This model offers better predictions than the regular LSTM. But it has the problem of learning dependencies and varied timescales due to the conventional initialization approach employed to control the distribution of forget gates. So we propose to initialize the value of forget gate activation by using the Kaiming Initialization function, and the algorithm is named Kai-Bi-LSTM.

In the testing phase, a sample image and the question are given to the system. The same process as in the training phase is done for the image and question. This feature and score value are given to the classifier. The result of the classifier is a score value corresponding to the answer. Then this score value and the question are matched with the LogishBERT dictionary. Based on that, a relevant answer is retrieved. The performance of the proposed system is compared with the existing methodology and the novelty of the proposed method is analysed by using the result parameters like Accuracy, Precision, Recall, F-Measure, etc. The block diagram of the proposed method is shown below in Fig. 2.

FRCNN and Kai-Bi LSTM were chosen for the visual question-answering system for healthcare imagery because they are more suited to accurate object localization, where the identification of specific structures or anomalies in medical images or imported images is crucial. This feature makes it possible to identify and categorize several items in one step, which is useful for tasks involving different anatomical structures. For improved performance, pre-trained CNN models like ResNet can be included. The VQA system's visual and textual features are organized using Kai-Bi-LSTM. It handles the verbal complexity of the intricate medical question and facilitates precise responses.

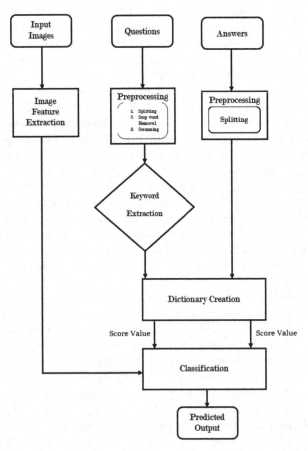

Fig. 2. Block Diagram of the Proposed Research Methodology

6 Experimental Setup

6.1 Dataset Collection

The ImageCLEF 2020 MedVQA dataset, which includes questions in the following four categories: modality, plan, organ system, and abnormality, is the basis for the research we propose. The VQG work included 80 radiology images for testing, 141 radiology photos with 164 questions, and more than 780 radiology images with 2,156 questions and answers linked to them for training. Comparison happens between the ImageCLEF 2020 MedVQA dataset and the ImageCLEF 2021 MedVQA dataset during the training and testing phases to find better accuracy.

6.2 Design Requirements

The intended Med-VQA system is implemented using the Python working platform. Popular high-level, all-purpose programming language Python Its syntax allows programmers to convey ideas more simply because it was designed with attention to code readability. Python is a programming language that integrates systems more effectively and operates swiftly. The virtual environment tool produces an isolated Python environment that is totally different from the system-wide Python environment (in the form of a directory).

7 Performance Evaluation Matrices

A campaign for evaluation, termed ImageCLEF 2019, is being planned by the CLEF initiative labs. Teams from all over the world are welcome to participate in the campaign's various research assignments. To produce a more focused set of questions for a suitable role evaluation, we initially thought of dividing the questions into four different categories based on: modality, plane, organ system, and abnormality. Variously challenging text creation and classification techniques were combined to create these categories. We especially selected medical questions that concentrated on a single characteristic in this second iteration of the VQA challenge (for instance, what is the main organ shown in this MRI? What kind of aircraft was used for this mammogram? This image has a flair, a t1 weight, or a t2 weight. What aspect of this ultrasonography is most worrisome? and this can be determined from the visual content without the need for further medical expertise or domain-specific inference. The VQA-Med-2019 Training Set: Most Frequent Answers section contains a list of the most popular responses for each category. The most common answers for each category are listed in the VQA-Med-2019 Training Set: Most Frequent Answers section. The test results were manually double-validated by a physician and a radiologist. 33 answers were altered, either by adding an optional element (8 answers), increasing the number of possible solutions (10 answers), or changing the automatic response (iii). The test had 15 corrected answers, or 3% of the total. The categories to which the corrected answers belong are Abnormality (8/125), Organ (6/125), and Plane (1/125). For questions with abnormalities, it is frequently necessary to change the diagnostic that is inferred by the problem depicted in the image. Given that both the training and validation sets were generated automatically, their error rates ought to be comparable. The test set consists of 500 medical images and 500 questions. The VQA-Med task summary focuses on abnormality-based questions [20] from the selected dataset (image CLEF 2021), which has a total of 4500 radiological images. The training dataset for the task also has 4500 questions and question-answer pairs. 500 radiological images and 500 questions about abnormalities make up this test set. Focusing on four various categories of questions, such as modality, planes, organ systems, and abnormalities, is part of our proposed approach (Fig. 3).

Total No. of Answers vs. Most Frequent Answers

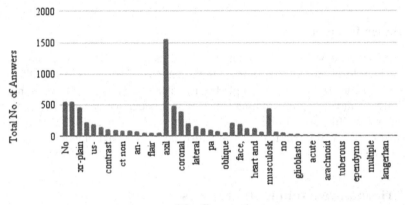

Fig. 3. Most frequent answers used in Modality, Plane, Organ system and Abnormality

7.1 Evaluation Matrices

A system, process, or strategy's performance, efficiency, and success are measured using evaluation metrics, which are accurate measurements or indicators. These metrics can be quantitative or qualitative in nature and are frequently based on key performance indicators (KPIs). In a wide variety of domains, including business, marketing, healthcare, education, and technology, evaluation measures are frequently utilized. They are employed to assess a strategy's or procedure's effectiveness, pinpoint areas that need improvement, and draw conclusions from the data gathered. Building computer vision systems that can perform a variety of tasks rather than being experts in just one (such as object recognition) is one of the key objectives of VQA research.

7.2 Accuracy

The Accuracy in Visual Question Answering (VQA) statistic calculates the proportion of questions in a dataset for which the model provides an accurate answer. In VQA, a system is presented with a question in natural language together with an image, and the system is supposed to respond appropriately. By dividing the total number of questions in the dataset by the number of questions with valid answers, the accuracy measure is often calculated. For example, if a VQA model was tested on a dataset of 1,000 photos and was able to correctly respond to 800 questions, its accuracy would be 80%. One of the most crucial evaluation criteria in VQA is accuracy, since it shows how well a model can comprehend an image's information and appropriately respond to inquiries about it. Other metrics, such as precision, recall, and F1 score, may also be employed to provide further insights into a model's performance, as accuracy alone may not necessarily give a complete view of a model's performance. Our model's accuracy was calculated to be about 50%.

7.3 BLEU Score

A higher score on the BLEU, which ranges from 0 to 1, indicates greater performance. While (BLEU score can offer some insight into the caliber of a VQA system's outcomes, it is crucial to be aware that the metric has several restrictions, such as failing to capture semantic similarity between answers and failing to take into account the variety of acceptable answers to a question. Therefore, it is advised to use a variety of evaluation metrics, such as BLEU, to have a thorough perspective on how well a VQA system is performing.

$$\min\left(1 - \frac{r}{c}, 0\right) + \sum_{n=1}^{4} \frac{logP_n}{4}$$

where: reference_length: the length of the reference answer output_length: the length of the generated answer bleu_ngram_weights: weights used for computing n-gram precisions pn: the n-gram precision for n-grams of length n in the generated answer n: the length of n-grams considered for computing the precision The weights used for computing n-gram precisions are typically uniform, but they can also be learned from data. For example, if we consider unigrams ($n = 1$) and bigrams ($n = 2$), the weights could be [0.5, 0.5] to give equal importance to both precisions. The revised n-gram precisions for each question in the dataset are combined to create the geometric mean of the BLEU score. The length difference between the reference and generated answers is taken into consideration when calculating the modified n-gram precision, which is calculated as the exponent of the arithmetic mean of the log-transformed n-gram precisions.

7.4 Result Analysis of First Phase of Dataset

See Figs. 4, 5, 6, 7 and 8.

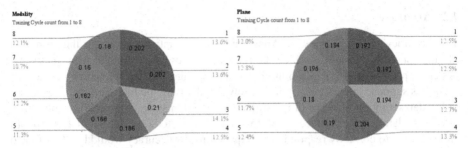

Fig. 4. Accuracy comparison on Modality   **Fig. 5.** Accuracy comparison on Plane

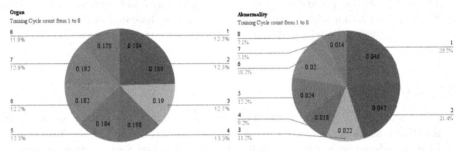

Fig. 6. Accuracy comparison on Organ   **Fig. 7.** Accuracy comparison on Abnormality

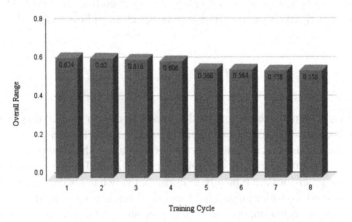

Fig. 8. Accuracy comparison for overall matrices

7.5 Result Set

If a VQA model is assessed using a dataset with image-related questions, the model's accuracy for questions pertaining to objects, characteristics, actions, and relationships should be determined individually. This can give insights into areas that require improvement and help identify the model's strengths and limitations when applied to various types of inquiries. Calculating an overall accuracy measure that reflects how well the

VQA model performed overall on the full dataset is also crucial. The percentage of questions that were properly answered out of all the questions in the dataset can be used to calculate this metric. The model's performance is summarized by the overall accuracy measure, which may also be used to compare the performance of various VQA models (Table 1).

Table 1. Three different Categories of radiology images with its related question and answer

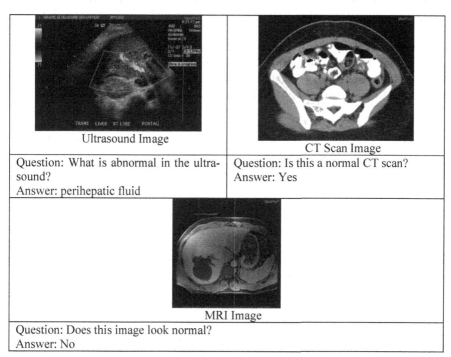

Ultrasound Image	CT Scan Image
Question: What is abnormal in the ultrasound? Answer: perihepatic fluid	Question: Is this a normal CT scan? Answer: Yes
MRI Image	
Question: Does this image look normal? Answer: No	

In summary, in order to offer a thorough assessment of the model's performance, the accuracy of a VQA model should be assessed for each type of question separately in addition to producing an overall accuracy score.

8 Conclusion

In conclusion, by giving medical practitioners automatic aid with the study of medical images, Visual Question Answering (VQA) systems have the potential to dramatically improve their abilities. These technologies are able to assist with medical condition diagnosis, increase practice efficiency, educate patients, support research and development, and enable telemedicine in remote locations. VQA systems are anticipated to grow increasingly complex and accurate as a result of the rapid Enhancement of computer vision capabilities and natural language processing, which will enhance patient outcomes and increase the effectiveness of medical treatment. As a result, VQA systems in medical imaging have a bright future and are likely to become an indispensable tool for healthcare practitioners in the years to come. The availability and quality of medical VQA datasets, the development and evaluation of medical VQA models, and the integration and use of medical VQA systems in clinical practices are some of the variables that will determine the future reach of medical VQA. Constructing extensive and comprehensive medical VQA datasets that encompass a range of modalities, diseases, ranging questions, and answers. Existing datasets frequently have size, breadth, or quality restrictions. Developing interpretable and comprehensible medical VQA models that may offer not only precise solutions but also argumentation and proof for their hypotheses. This could improve the confidence and efficiency of medical VQA systems. To increase the robustness and generalizability of medical VQA models, domain expertise and outside data are incorporated. Knowledge graphs, ontologies, or other sources of medical information can be used for this.

Conflict of Interest Statement.   There are no declared conflicts of interest between the authors and the subject matter of this paper.

References

1. Liu, S., Zhang, X., Zhou, X., Yang, J.: BPI-MVQA a bi-branch Model for medical visual question answering. BMC Med. Imaging **22**(1), 1–19 (2022)
2. Lubna, A., Kalady, S., Lijiya, A.: MoBVQA a modality based medical image visual question System. In: 2019 IEEE Region 10 Conference, TENCON 2019, 17–20 October 2019, Kochi, India. IEEE (2019)
3. Muhammad, F., Abbas, Z.H., Abbas, G., Jiao, L.: Decoupled downlink-uplink coverage analysis with interference management for enriched heterogeneous cellular networks. IEEE Access **4**, 6250–6260 (2016)
4. Sharma, D., Purushotham, S., Reddy, C.K.: MedFuseNet an attention based multimodal deep learning model for visual question answering in the medical domain. Sci. Rep. **11**(1), 1–18 (2021)
5. Ren, F., Zhou, Y.: CGMVQA a new classification and generative model for medical visual question answering. IEEE Access **8**, 50626–50636 (2020)
6. Bazi, Y., Al Rahhal, M.M., Bashmal, L., Zuair, M.: Vision–language model for visual question answering in medical imagery. Bioengineering **10**, 380 (2023)
7. Li, L., Lei, J., Gan, Z., Liu, J.: Adversarial VQA: a new benchmark for evaluating the robustness of VQA models. In: Proceedings of the IEEE/CVF International Conference on Computer Vision, Montreal, QC, Canada, 10–17 October 2021, pp. 2022–2031 (2021)
8. Devlin, J., Chang, M.-W., Lee, K., Toutanova, K.: BERT: pre-training of deep bidirectional transformers for language understanding. arXiv arXiv:1810.04805 (2019)
9. He, K., Zhang, X., Ren, S., Sun, J.: Deep residual learning for image recognition. In: Proceedings of the IEEE Conference on Computer Vision and Pattern Recognition, pp. 770–778 (2016)
10. Srinivasan, K., et al.: Performance comparison of deep CNN models for detecting driver's distraction. CMC-Comput. Mater. Continua. **68**(3), 4109–4124 (2021)
11. Cho, K., Van Merriënboer, B., Gulcehre, C., Bahdanau, D., Bougares, F., Schwenk, H., Bengio, Y.: Learning phrase representations using RNN encoder-decoder for statistical machine translation. arXiv preprint arXiv:1406.1078 (2014)

12. Lee, J., et al.: BioBERT: a pre-trained biomedical language representation model for biomedical text mining. Bioinformatics **36**(4), 1234–1240 (2020)
13. Devlin, J., Chang, M.-W., Lee, K., Toutanova, K.: BERT: pre-training of deep bidirectional transformers for language understanding. arXiv preprint arXiv:1810.04805 (2018)
14. Peng, Y., Liu, F., Rosen, M.P.: UMass at ImageCLEF medical visual question answering (Med-VQA) 2018 Task. In: CLEF (Working Notes) (2018)
15. Zhejiang University at ImageCLEF 2019 Visual Question Answering in the Medical Domain (2019)
16. Kornuta, T., Rajan, D., Shivade, C., Asseman, A., Ozcan, A.S.: Leveraging medical visual question answering with supporting facts. arXiv preprint arXiv:1905.12008 (2019)
17. Liao, Z., Wu, Q., Shen, C., Van Den Hengel, A., Verjans, J.: AIML at VQA-Med 2020: knowledge inference via a skeleton-based sentence mapping approach for medical domain visual question answering (2020)
18. Al-Sadi, A., Hana'Al-Theiabat, Al-Ayyoub, M.: The inception team at VQA-Med 2020: Pretrained VGG with data augmentation for medical VQA and VQG. In: CLEF (Working Notes) (2020)
19. Zhan, L.-M., Liu, B., Fan, L., Chen, J., Wu, X.-M.: Medical visual question answering via conditional reasoning. In: Proceedings of the 28th ACM International Conference on Multimedia, pp. 2345–2354 (2020)
20. Abacha, A.B., Hasan, S.A., Datla, V.V., Liu, J., Demner-Fushman, D., M¨uller, H.: VQA-Med: overview of the medical visual question answering task at ImageCLEF 2019. In: CLEF (Working Notes) (2019)

Author Index

B
Bakane, Pramar   14

C
Chandrashekara, S.   55
Chaware, Anita   1

G
Gawade, Sushopti   87

J
Jaju, S. B.   14
Jiang, Jiaxin   39

M
Mallikarjunaswamy, M. S.   55
Melvin, Y. I. Jinesh   87
Mishra, Jitendra Kumar   71

P
Patel, Rupa   1
Pimple, Jagdish F.   71
Praveen, P.   55

S
Sharma, Avinash   71
Shrimali, Mukesh   87

Z
Zhou, Yanhui   39

S. Ponnusamy and V. R. Bora (Eds.): AIBTR 2023, CCIS 1987, p. 103, 2024.
https://doi.org/10.1007/978-3-031-49454-3

Printed in the United States
by Baker & Taylor Publisher Services